AF255833

WINNING THE
WAR WITHIN

WINNING THE WAR WITHIN

SPIRITUAL WARFARE & SOUL CARE

*A Handbook for Conquering
Spiritual and Emotional Battles Through
the Power of the Holy Spirit*

Winning the War Within | Spiritual Warfare & Soul Care
A handbook for conquering spiritual and emotional battles through the power of the Holy Spirit
by Dr. Robert Tucker

Published by
Living Free Institute
28481 Rancho California Road, Suite 101
Temecula, CA 92590
United States

This book is intended for educational and spiritual growth purposes. It is not intended to replace professional medical, psychological, or legal advice. Readers are encouraged to seek qualified professional guidance where appropriate.

ISBN: 978-1-936451-11-1

Printed in the United States of America

"Then you will know (ginōskō) the truth, and the truth will set you free." —John 8:32

Table of Contents

Introduction..Page 9

Chapter 1 – The Power of Knowing ....Page 15

Chapter 2 – Three-Part Beings - Body, Soul, and Spirit .... Page 35

Chapter 3 – Fragmentation of the Soul .... Page 67

Chapter 4 – The Invisible Conflict ....Page 81

Chapter 5 – The Spiritual Realm is at the Door.................. Page 91

Chapter 6 – Cleansing of the Temple .... Page 103

Chapter 7 – God as Judge and Redeemer ....Page 119

Chapter 8 – Discerning Spiritual Conditions ....Page 131

Chapter 9 – Filled, Empowered, and Commissioned ....Page 155

Chapter 10 – Deliverance as a Ministry ....Page 173

Chapter 11 – Importance of Prayer and Meditation ....Page 191

Chapter 12 – Battle Ready & Equipped to Win................Page 207

Resources ....Page 229

INTRODUCTION

Robert Tucker's life reflects a profound journey shaped by personal struggle and the transformative intervention of the Holy Spirit. Set free and commissioned to share that same freedom with others, Robert's story is one of restoration and divine redirection. From childhood, he displayed a unique gifting and passion for building and restoring physical structures. For more than forty years, he worked as a successful licensed Building Contractor in the State of California, constructing, remodeling and restoring commercial, industrial, residential, and historical properties. Yet, in time, the Lord called him away from building earthly structures to build lives for His Kingdom. What began as his motto in the building industry—"We Bring It Back to Life"—evolved into a deeper spiritual truth: "He Brings Us Back to Life."

As the founder and director of New Life Spirit Recovery, Spirit of Life Ministries, Tucker Counseling Services, Spirit of Life Recovery Church, Gracious Giver Church, and Living Free Institute, Robert has dedicated his life to helping individuals break free from unhealthy behaviors, oppression, strongholds, and soul ties. Through a Christ-centered approach—integrated with more than twenty years of clinical experience and over twenty-five years in ministry—he guides others toward genuine healing and lasting transformation. His personal journey, from overcoming his own struggles to becoming a respected leader in the field, stands as a powerful testament to faith, perseverance, and purpose.

This book delves into the different influences that shape our lives, showing how they can either obstruct or facilitate the fulfillment of our God-given, predestined purpose. By exploring both seen and unseen forces, it offers a thorough understanding of the factors affecting human behavior and spiritual growth, providing valuable insights on overcoming challenges and aligning our lives with God's divine plan.

At some point in this imperfect world, God's perfect plan has been interrupted, hindered, and distorted by various influences and external forces. These disruptions can begin as early as conception and are often shaped by external sources such as parents, family members, friends, peers, environmental conditions, the broader community, and the unseen principalities and powers described in Ephesians 6.

The reality that God's perfect plan can be hindered by both external and internal influences is a profound truth. It highlights the importance of discerning these influences and taking intentional steps to properly address them. When left unresolved, they can impede a person's ability to fully align with and walk in God's perfect purpose for their life.

If you're interested in learning more about Robert Tucker's work or the principles he shares, his book and programs offer valuable insights that can be truly transformative and life-changing.

WHY A THEOCENTRIC HEALING APPROACH

Theocentric counseling is Christ-centered counseling—Biblical truth imparted under the guidance and direction of the Holy Spirit. The Holy Spirit must be involved because only our Creator has the ability and power to realign us with His predestined perfect purpose.

The challenges people face are often complex and multi-faceted, requiring a holistic approach for true and lasting change. Our goal is not simply behavior modification, but authentic transformation from the inside out. Psychology—the study of the mind—offers valuable insight into the root causes of many struggles, since the mind is often where these issues first take hold. Theocentric, Christ-centered counseling thoughtfully integrates psychological understanding with biblical truth, addressing the full complexity of an individual's life. This approach neither distorts psychology nor conforms to humanistic ideologies; rather, it provides spiritual and emotional support firmly grounded in the Word of God.

Theocentric Christian counseling emphasizes the role of the spirit and the effects of soul wounds, recognizing how both shape memory, emotions, and decision-making. Its ultimate aim is spiritual freedom and the renewal of a healthy mind, achieved by integrating the healing power of the Great Physician with a Christ-centered therapeutic approach.

Psychology is the study of the soul, mind and behavior. It seeks to understand how people think (cognition), feel (emotion), act (behavior), relate to others (social psychology), and develop and change over time (developmental psychology).

The Theocentric Christian counselor recognizes the intricate workings of the mind—how it is shaped by influences and, in turn, shapes behavior. The counseling process begins by gathering information and assessing how a person thinks, feels, and acts. This approach considers a broad spectrum of factors, including an individual's history, perception, cognition, emotions, personality, and overall mental health.

Most secular approaches often exclude the spiritual components that lie at the root of many struggles, and inevitably overlook the true source of healing. Only the Holy Spirit has the power to expose, reveal, remove, and restore. He equips the Christian counselor with discernment, granting insight beyond what is visible to the natural eye. While outward behaviors and manifestations can be observed, the unseen spiritual influences and inner brokenness often remain hidden. When these areas are properly assessed and addressed, genuine freedom becomes possible. This underscores the vital role of counseling in soul care, spiritual deliverance, discipleship, and ongoing growth in Christ.

The Bible underscores the importance of seeking wise counsel. God Himself is described as "wonderful in counsel" (Isaiah 28:29), and Jesus is proclaimed the "Wonderful Counselor" (Isaiah 9:6). The Holy Spirit is likewise called the Counselor (John 14:16, 26; 16:7), guiding believers into all truth (1 Corinthians 2:10; Luke 12:12). This biblical foundation highlights the vital role of counseling within the church, offering both spiritual and practical guidance to help believers face personal struggles and grow in their faith.

The secular and biblical worldviews often clash, remaining as two distinct approaches to treatment. Yet the Theocentric Counselor recognizes the need to integrate them, offering a holistic approach that addresses the whole person. The theocentric model considers every aspect of the individual being treated—spirit, soul, and body—while grounding care in Christ-centered truth.

The typical secular approach focuses on self-actualization and coping with life's challenges through human reasoning and emotional strategies. Solutions are often rooted in man's own understanding, with the belief that healing is found within the individual. Emphasis is placed on mental and emotional techniques to manage symptoms and encourage personal growth.

Ultimately, success is defined by well-being achieved through self-will and self-discovery, rather than reliance on any external or spiritual source. In this sense, it is behavior modification rather than Holy Spirit–guided transformation.

The Theocentric, Christ-centered approach emphasizes transformation into the likeness of Christ, rather than merely modifying or managing behavior and emotions. Its solutions are firmly grounded in Scripture and divine truth, with the conviction that true healing is the work of the Holy Spirit within the individual. This model addresses the whole person—spirit, soul, and relationships—in alignment with God's perfect design.

True success is not measured by self-fulfillment, but by becoming whole in Christ: living in freedom, walking in purpose, and experiencing restored relationships with God and others. In essence, Theocentric counseling is Christ-centered, Spirit-led, and transformation-focused. It prioritizes genuine inner change accomplished by the Holy Spirit in the life of a believer, rather than settling for symptom relief or behavior modification. The more intentionally we draw near to Jesus, desiring to be like Him, the more we are transformed into His image.

My prayer is that your experience reading this book will be truly life-changing—bringing freedom, equipping you to inspire others, and enabling you to deliver hope and healing to all whom God places within your sphere of influence.

Chapter 1
THE POWER OF KNOWING

"Now the Lord is the Spirit, and where the Spirit of the Lord is, there is freedom."—2 Corinthians 3:17 (NIV)

You were made to be free, and that truth has been stamped into the very fabric of who you are. Before you ever breathed your first breath, God had already written His own life into your DNA. His intention was never that you should be bound by fear, crippled by shame, or trapped in invisible chains. From the very beginning, His design was wholeness—life marked by love, anchored in purpose, and overflowing with the abundance that only He can give.

And yet, if we are honest, the life we experience rarely matches that design. Pain we never asked for leaves its scars. Loneliness settles into spaces that were meant for connection. We feel a disconnect inside ourselves, and sometimes even from God. These struggles are not accidents or random disruptions; they are the visible evidence of a greater conflict—one that rages not only in the culture around us, but in the unseen places of our own hearts and minds.

This battle cannot be measured by our natural senses. You won't pick it up with sight, sound, or touch, but its effects are undeniable. You feel its pressure in the temptations that seem impossible to escape, in the accusations that echo inside your thoughts, and in the fear that keeps you from stepping forward into the life you know you were made for. The conflict is real, and it presses against us day and night.

But here is the truth: no one enters a war unarmed and expects to walk away victorious. You cannot stand before an enemy determined to destroy you and hope to triumph with empty hands. Victory comes only when the power within you is greater than the power coming against you.

And the good news is this—God has already placed that power inside you. Through Christ, the Holy Spirit dwells in you, equipping you with authority and strength far greater than anything the enemy can muster.

The Christian life is not about surviving a hostile world until we can escape it. It is about learning to walk in the authority of the Spirit, to rise above fear and accusation, and to live the fullness of the freedom we were created for. This is not the story of barely making it—it is the story of sons and daughters of God stepping into the life they were always meant to live.

This book is about that battle. But even more, it is about living in His freedom.

EQUIPPED FOR VICTORY

Like every battle, readiness, resources, and proper equipping are essential. No soldier steps onto a battlefield ill-equipped and without weapons, expecting to survive. In the same way, we cannot stand firm in our own strength. Victory is never achieved through willpower or determination alone—it comes when the power of the Holy Spirit living within overpowers what is coming against us.

Still, many of us misidentify the enemy. We assume the struggle lies with another person, a broken relationship, or an unrelenting circumstance. In our ignorance, we often turn the blame inward or cast it on others, unaware that there is another entity at work. The truth runs deeper, and Scripture speaks plainly:

"For our struggle is not against flesh and blood, but against the rulers, against the authorities, against the powers of this dark world and against the spiritual forces of evil in the heavenly realms." (Ephesians 6:12, NIV)

The real war is not against people. It is not against the boss who mistreats us, the spouse who misunderstands us, or the friend who betrays us. The true battle is against an unseen enemy—working beneath the surface through lies, accusations, unhealed wounds, and strongholds buried deep within the heart. His purpose is clear: to distort how we see ourselves, how we see others, how we see God, and ultimately, how we live our lives.

THE WORD AS OUR FIRST WEAPON

The first and most important weapon we hold is the very blueprint for life: God's Word. It reveals what is unfolding even when our natural senses remain silent. Scripture describes it as "living and active, sharper than any double-edged sword" (Hebrews 4:12), able to cut through confusion and expose the truth at the deepest level.

Yet living out that truth is not always simple. Under the pressures of daily life, the Bible can feel distant, difficult to understand, or nearly impossible to apply. That is because we were never meant to reduce the Word of God to a manual we try to figure out with human reasoning. The Word is not information—it is revelation. It is not only text on a page—it is the living testimony of a living Savior.

We are called to abide in relationship with Jesus, who is Himself the Word made flesh (John 1:14). As we walk with Him, the Holy Spirit breathes life into His written Word, moving it from Logos to *Rhema*, transforming us from the inside out until His likeness becomes our own. The Bible in your hand becomes power in your life when it is carried by the Holy Spirit into the broken places of your soul.

And this is where the battle is most fierce. Every one of us carries wounds, heartaches, disappointments, and distortions of truth—open spaces in our hearts where the enemy seeks to establish footholds. These inner battlegrounds are where lies speak louder than truth and fear feels stronger than faith. But it is precisely here, in the broken places, that God's resources prove most powerful. When we yield to Him, His Spirit overtakes what we cannot fix in ourselves. His strength fills the gaps where ours collapses.

The more we understand about this inner war—how it began, where it strikes, and why it lingers—the more we can cooperate with the Spirit's powerful work in us. Recognizing the enemy's strategy is not about giving him attention; it is about applying the right resources to the right places so we can walk in lasting freedom.

There comes a moment for every believer when freedom must be pursued. It is the moment we realize that our inner world is not aligned with peace, love, and the deep assurance of wholeness.

If we ignore the call to healing, we remain stuck in cycles—striving for freedom, tasting it briefly, only to feel it slip away again.

Transformation is not a single event; it is an ongoing process of anchoring ourselves in God's truth through the indwelling presence of the Holy Spirit, deepening our relationship with Jesus, and refusing to reopen doors to spiritual opposition or unhealthy influences. True freedom is not a destination we reach once and for all, but a condition of the heart—a way of living. It requires daily dependence on and interaction with the Holy Spirit, allowing His Word to come alive within us to comfort, empower, reshape our thinking, heal our wounds, and transform us from the inside out.

This is the journey before us. Together, we will take a closer look at the war within, learn to see beyond the limits of human intellect, and step into a Christ-centered perspective—one that calls us out of striving and into the help and healing only His Spirit can bring.

HOW WE FIGHT TO WIN

We have far more power than we could ever comprehend. God has already given us everything we need to overcome. Yet so often, we fail to recognize this power and authority because we listen more closely to the standards and ways of the world than to the heart of God:

> *"Do not conform to the pattern of this world, but be transformed by the renewing of your mind. Then you will be able to test and approve what God's will is—his good, pleasing and perfect will." – (Romans 12:2).*

Salvation—also called regeneration—is the step into a personal relationship with Jesus Christ. It is essential before we can move forward in our faith journey. Attending church and learning about God are valuable, but they do not make someone a Christian any more than sitting in a garage makes you a car. At some point, each person must choose to accept Jesus' gift of salvation and commit to building an intimate relationship with Him:

> *"For it is by grace you have been saved, through faith—and this is not from yourselves, it is the gift of God— not by works, so that no one can boast." – (Ephesians 2:8–9).*

Salvation is not merely an emotional experience—it is a transaction of the heart. In that moment, we agree with God that we cannot do life on our own and that we need His grace to be transformed into His likeness. We surrender our lives to Him, allowing ourselves to be both transformed by His power and used for His purposes.

Jesus made this process simple: believe in Him, trust His promises, and accept the grace He offers. Scripture promises:

> *"If you declare with your mouth, 'Jesus is Lord,' and believe in your heart that God raised him from the dead, you will be saved." (Romans 10:9, NIV)*

From that moment on, we begin to experience the fullness of life in relationship with Him. Yet salvation is only the beginning. Growing in that relationship is where the deeper work of transformation begins.

BEYOND A CHECKLIST

That first "yes" to Jesus opens the door to a lifelong journey of reconciling what the world has taught us with what God declares is true. Transformation requires a redeemed and renewed heart, one willing to let go of old patterns and step into the new life God has designed.

This transition to living by faith in Jesus is not about following a formula or completing a checklist. It is about receiving a revelation of the power we have been given as children of God—the resurrection power, the *dunamis* power that raised Jesus from the dead and now lives within us (Ephesians 1:18–20). We must learn to access and walk in this power if we are to fulfill all God has for us.

> *"I pray that the eyes of your heart may be enlightened in order that you may know the hope to which he has called you, the riches of his glorious inheritance in his holy people, and his incomparably great power for us who believe. That power is the same as the mighty strength he exerted when he raised Christ from the dead and seated him at his right hand in the heavenly realms." (Ephesians 1:18–20 NIV)*

As representatives of the Kingdom of God, the question is not merely whether we teach about Jesus, but whether He is teaching through us. Only the latter has the power to truly change lives and produce lasting transformation. This is why understanding the deeper meaning of new wine in new wineskins is so crucial—Jesus is doing a new thing.

Scripture consistently contrasts teaching empowered by the Holy Spirit with teaching driven by human effort. Paul explains that God makes His servants ministers "not of the letter but of the Spirit; for the letter kills, but the Spirit gives life," revealing that truth detached from the Spirit can wound rather than heal. Likewise, Jesus rebuked religious leaders who knew the Scriptures intellectually yet missed their purpose, declaring that although they diligently studied the Scriptures, they refused to come to Him for life.

> *"You study the Scriptures diligently because you think that in them you have eternal life. These are the very Scriptures that testify about me, yet you refuse to come to me to have life."* *(John 5:39–40 NIV)*

Flesh-led teaching exalts knowledge, rules, and outward conformity, often producing pride or condemnation, whereas Spirit-led teaching flows from surrender, pointing people to Christ and producing freedom and inner transformation. As Paul writes:

> *"The person without the Spirit does not accept the things that come from the Spirit of God... because they are discerned only through the Spirit"* *(1 Corinthians 2:14).*

In contrast, Spirit-led ministry imparts life, aligns hearts with God's truth, and results in genuine change, because:

> *"Now the Lord is the Spirit, and where the Spirit of the Lord is, there is freedom."* *(2 Corinthians 3:17 NIV)*

Religion is humanity's attempt to strive for God's approval. Salvation, however, is not about earning approval—it is about receiving Jesus Christ, who is our approval before the Father. This establishes a relationship built on love rather than performance, and on God's sufficiency rather than our own.

You cannot pour new wine into old wineskins; the life of the New Covenant cannot be contained within old systems, mind-sets, or law-based approaches. New wine requires new wineskins.

Resurrection life cannot be carried by unrenewed hearts, religious performance, or law-centered thinking.

"And no one pours new wine into old wineskins. Otherwise, the new wine will burst the skins… No, new wine must be poured into new wineskins." (Luke 5:37–38 NIV)

Born-again, Spirit-filled, Spirit-led believers are the new wineskins, and the New Covenant—established through Christ's blood and empowered by the Holy Spirit—is the new wine.

"Not that we are competent in ourselves to claim anything for ourselves, but our competence comes from God. He has made us competent as ministers of a new covenant—not of the letter but of the Spirit; for the letter kills, but the Spirit gives life." – (2 Corinthians 3:5-6 NIV).

KNOWING ABOUT VS. KNOWING GOD

For many, the struggle to walk in relationship with God arises from attempting to grasp One who cannot be measured by sight or sound. In response, it can feel easier to rely on lists, rules, or systems. Yet God's Word was never intended to be reduced to a "to-do list." When we attempt to live the Christian life in our own strength, we quickly discover its impossibility. If it were achievable through human effort, the cross would not have been necessary. Jesus desires an up-close, personal, and intimate relationship with each of those He has created.

The Greek language highlights the difference well. The word *oida*, for the most part, refers to intellectual understanding—facts or information about God. This is like reading the Bible as a history book: accurate, informative, but impersonal. We may respect what we learn, but it doesn't connect us to a living relationship.

By contrast, the word *ginōskō* refers to experiential, relational knowledge—knowing someone through lived experience. This is the kind of knowing that transforms hearts, minds, and lives. It is the intimacy that only comes from walking with someone, being close to them, and sharing life together:

> *"I want to know Christ—yes, to know the power of his resurrection and participation in his sufferings, becoming like him in his death." (Philippians 3:10).*

To illustrate, *oida* is like reading about Abraham Lincoln in a textbook. *Ginōskō* is like Abraham Lincoln walking into your home, sitting with you, and doing life side by side. The difference is that vast—it is the difference between knowing about God and actually knowing Him.

Transformation comes only through relationship—by personally experiencing His love, His grace, and His presence. Scripture declares:

> *"Everyone who loves has been born of God and knows [ginōskō] God." (1 John 4:7–8, NIV)*

This is what sets the Christian life apart from religion. It is not about outward performance or surface obedience, but about inward communion—relationship and transformation that flow from truly knowing Him, walking with Him, and living daily in His love. Jesus makes this distinction unmistakably clear when He says:

> *"Not everyone who says to me, 'Lord, Lord,' will enter the kingdom of heaven, but only the one who does the will of my Father who is in heaven. Many will say to me on that day, 'Lord, Lord, did we not prophesy in your name and in your name drive out demons and in your name perform many miracles?' Then I will tell them plainly, 'I never knew you. Away from me, you evildoers!'" (Matthew 7:21–23 NIV)*

When Jesus said, "I never knew you," how could this be possible since He is all-knowing? The answer lies in the meaning of the word "know." The Greek word used in this context is *ginosko*, which refers not merely to intellectual knowledge but to intimate, relational knowing. It is the same word Jesus used when speaking of His relationship with the Father, and the same word used to describe Mary not "knowing" Joseph until after Jesus was conceived.

These people displayed outward signs of ministry—prophesying, casting out demons, performing miracles—yet Jesus declared, "I never knew you," because they lacked true relationship with Him. They were doing His work for Him, but without Him. Ministry without intimacy with Christ is empty. Jesus said, "Away from me, I never knew you" as a warning that outward religion and impressive works mean nothing without a true relationship with Him. He is looking for hearts that belong to Him, not just hands that perform in His name.

JESUS' MISSION AND ASCENSION

Jesus' departure signified the completion of His earthly ministry. His death, resurrection, and ascension fulfill the purpose of His coming to atone for sins, provide a way for humanity to be reconciled with God, and set the stage for the recovery process to begin.

By returning to the Father, Jesus was glorified. His ascension marked His exaltation to a place of authority and power at the right hand of God.

> *"..which He brought about in Christ, when He raised Him from the dead and seated Him at His right hand in the heavenly places, far above all rule and authority and power and dominion, and every name that is named, not only in this age but also in the one to come. And He put all things in subjection under His feet, and gave Him as head over all things to the church, which is His body, the fullness of Him who fills all in all." (Eph. 1:20)*

Before His departure, Jesus passed the baton to all who would believe, commissioning them to carry forward His mission. He promised to send a Helper—the Holy Spirit—to teach them, remind them, comfort them, and guide them all the way to the finish line. Every believer has a God-ordained, purposeful role in His redemptive plan, and it is only through the presence and power of the Holy Spirit that this calling can be fully realized. Jesus said:

> *"Nevertheless, I tell you the truth; It is expedient for you that I go away: for if I go not away, the Comforter will not come unto you; but if I depart, I will send Him unto you." (John 16:7 KJV)*

Jesus said to His followers:

> *"But you will receive power when the Holy Spirit comes on you; and you will be my witnesses in Jerusalem, and in all Judea and Samaria, and to the ends of the earth." (Acts 1:8 NIV)*

THE WORK OF THE HOLY SPIRIT

The question is this: How can a human being, with limited human understanding, come to know an invisible God at such a deep level? How do we move beyond merely knowing about Him to truly knowing Him in a personal and intimate way?

Jesus did not come only to provide a salvation experience and then leave us to figure everything out on our own. He made us a promise. He would not leave us as orphans. He would send us a Helper—the Holy Spirit—who would dwell with us and in us, empowering all who believe.

At Pentecost, the Holy Spirit came to dwell within all true believers, providing a continuous, internal presence of God. This indwelling was new compared to Old Testament times, where the Spirit's presence was often temporary or situational, and for the most part, manifested through Prophets.

The Holy Spirit would now lead all believers into all truth, teaching them and reminding them of Jesus' words. This was crucial for the disciples to understand and continue Jesus' teachings after His departure as He commanded in His Great Commission.

The Holy Spirit, the Advocate is not merely an idea, an expression of God, or a distant influence. He is God. He is a Person of the Trinity whose role is to dwell within us and imprint the truths of Scripture onto the very fabric of our souls, so that we encounter God tangibly rather than merely intellectually.

"But the Advocate, the Holy Spirit, whom the Father will send in my name, will teach you all things and will remind you of everything I have said to you." — John 14:26

Notice what Jesus said: the Spirit would come to teach, remind, and guide. He didn't say, "If I don't go away, the Bible won't come," because the Scriptures were already being written on scrolls and established as God's inspired Word. What Jesus emphasized was that the very Author and Inspirer of the Word—

the Holy Spirit—would come to live within us. His purpose was not only that we might know truth, but that we might become and live that truth through His indwelling presence.

THE SPIRIT'S ROLE

Scripture describes the Spirit as Advocate, Comforter, Helper, Teacher, Guide, and Protector. These are not abstract titles. They are deeply personal roles that reveal His intimate involvement in our daily lives. The Spirit empowers believers to live by God's strength rather than their own. He brings clarity in confusion, courage in weakness, and power in the face of spiritual opposition. Through Him, the presence of Jesus continues to dwell with us—guiding, correcting, and equipping us for the battles we face.

Without Him, we cannot truly understand the ways of God or be transformed by His power. As Paul wrote:

> *"The Spirit searches all things, even the deep things of God… we have received the Spirit who is from God, so that we may understand what God has freely given us." (1 Corinthians 2:10–12 NIV)*

A CALL TO GREATER WORKS

Jesus made a staggering statement to His disciples:

> *"Very truly I tell you, whoever believes in me will do the works I have been doing, and they will do even greater things than these, because I am going to the Father. And I will do whatever you ask in my name, so that the Father may be glorified in the Son. You may ask me for anything in my name, and I will do it." (John 14:12–14 NIV)*

How could such a thing be possible—that ordinary people could do greater works than Jesus? The answer is simple but profound: Jesus established a culture of power and then gave us the enablement, in "His name", and by His Spirit, to walk in it.

Humanity without the Spirit is limited to human interpretation, ideas, and solutions. But through Jesus, we have access to the Spirit of Almighty God. The same Spirit who raised Christ from the dead now lives in every true believer. This is not theory; it is the foundation of the Christian life. The Spirit of God empowers us not only to survive but to live transformed and to transform the world around us.

"And if the Spirit of him who raised Jesus from the dead is living in you, he who raised Christ from the dead will also give life to your mortal bodies because of his Spirit who lives in you." (Romans 8:11 NIV)

THE WORD IS ALIVE

With this in mind, we recognize that God has given us the Bible as our guide. The written Word shapes our theology—our understanding of who God is, how He works, and what He expects.

But God did not stop there. He gave us something even greater: Jesus Himself, the living Word, and the indwelling presence of the Holy Spirit. This means that in the life of every true believer, there are two dimensions of the Word working together—His written Word that informs us, and His living Word that transforms us.

Logos refers to the written Word—the entire body of Scripture revealing God's eternal truth. *Logos is* the unchanging message of God's will, the foundation of our faith, and the framework for understanding His nature. It is the anchor that secures us to what is true regardless of circumstance, opinion, culture, or emotion.

"In the beginning was the Word, and the Word was with God, and the Word was God." (John 1:1 NIV)

Rhema, on the other hand, refers to the personal, spoken Word of the Holy Spirit within our hearts (Ephesians 6:17). *Rhema* is when God's truth comes alive in a specific moment—when a verse seems to leap off the page, when conviction grips our spirit, when confusion breaks into clarity. *Rhema* is not a new truth apart from Scripture; it is the Spirit breathing life into the written Word, applying it to our situation in real time.

"For the word of God is alive and active. Sharper than any double-edged sword, it penetrates even to dividing soul and spirit, joints and marrow; it judges the thoughts and attitudes of the heart." (Hebrews 4:12 NIV)

When we talk about "the Word," we must understand both dimensions working together. Logos provides the firm foundation—the accurate, tangible account of God and His ways. *Rhema* makes that Word personal and active, shaping our decisions, bringing conviction, and leading us into deeper intimacy with Him.

One without the other leaves us incomplete. If we only lean on *Logos*, we risk knowing truth but never experiencing its power. If we only chase *Rhema*, we risk drifting into experience without the anchor of Scripture. But when *Logos* and *Rhema* work together, we encounter a vibrant, personal, transforming relationship with God—one that is rooted in His eternal Word and alive through His Spirit.

HEALING AND LIVING OUT FREEDOM

To begin this journey, we must understand that stepping into a faith-based life requires more than good intentions or religious activity. It calls for moving beyond the limitations of human reasoning into a life fully activated by the Holy Spirit. Living a Christ-centered life is not about finding balance between flesh and Spirit—as if the two could coexist effectively in harmony—but about complete surrender to Jesus. It is walking closely with Him and allowing the Holy Spirit to empower every step we take. There is no middle ground. Without growth in the Spirit, we remain vulnerable to other spirit influences—the pull of the flesh and the deception of the world.

> *"So I say, walk by the Spirit, and you will not gratify the desires of the flesh. For the flesh desires what is contrary to the Spirit, and the Spirit what is contrary to the flesh. They are in conflict with each other, so that you are not to do whatever you want. But if you are led by the Spirit, you are not under the law. (Galatians 5:16–18 NIV)*

Moving from head knowledge to heart transformation requires an intentional choice. It is not enough to learn facts about God or memorize verses without experiencing their power.

Transformation comes when we surrender self, receive His wisdom into our hearts and allow Him to reshape us from within. Paul puts it this way:

> *"Do not conform to the pattern of this world, but be transformed by the renewing of your mind." (Romans 12:2 NIV)*

The word "transformed" points to a true metamorphosis—a radical change from one form to another. Just as a caterpillar becomes a butterfly, we are called to move from the old life of self-will into a new life of surrender, dependence, and trust in Christ. The more time we spend in His presence, the more we will become like Him.

SPIRITUAL WISDOM

In this place of surrender, we gain access to something the world can never provide: spiritual wisdom. This wisdom is not abstract theory; it is divine insight applied to the real situations of our lives. Grounded in God's truth and empowered by the Spirit, it enables us to make choices that align with His will and purposes.

> *"If any of you lacks wisdom, you should ask God, who gives generously to all without finding fault, and it will be given to you." (James 1:5 NIV)*

> *"For the Lord gives wisdom; from his mouth come knowledge and understanding." (Proverbs 2:6 NIV)*

Worldly wisdom leans on human reasoning, temporary fixes, and self-sufficiency. Spiritual wisdom flows from humility, trust in God, and reliance on His voice. One keeps us trapped in cycles of striving; the other leads us into freedom and clarity.

The wisdom given by the Spirit equips us to live in a way that reflects God's character. It steadies us with peace when circumstances are shaken, provides clarity when choices seem uncertain, and empowers us to walk confidently in the purpose God has set before us. More than simply shifting our perspective, this wisdom transforms how we think, feel, act, and respond to life's challenges. Again, we are reminded that the Bible calls it a renewing of the mind:

> *"Do not conform to the pattern of this world, but be transformed by the renewing of your mind. Then you will be able to test and approve what God's will is—His good, pleasing and perfect will." — (Romans 12:2 NIV)*

ACCEPTING THE OFFER

It can be difficult to develop a spiritual perspective when we live in a world that has inherently rejected God. Before you go deeper in your own journey, remember this: the world rejects Him because it cannot see Him or understand Him. That rejection should not surprise us—it is the natural response of a world bound by its own reasoning and blinded to the Spirit's reality.

> *"The world cannot accept him, because it neither sees him nor knows him. But you know him, for he lives with you and will be in you." (John 14:17 NIV)*

Even within the Church, some choose to follow Christ yet remain only at the surface level of Logos—knowing the written Word—while resisting the *Rhema* aspect of God's truth. As a result, many distort or even deny foundational doctrines such as the Trinity or the divinity of Jesus. This highlights the danger of relying solely on head knowledge without entering into a genuine, transformative relationship with Him.

> *"The person without the Spirit does not accept the things that come from the Spirit of God but considers them foolishness, and cannot understand them because they are discerned only through the Spirit." (1 Corinthians 2:14 NIV)*

But if you sense God inviting you now, consider it the opportunity of a lifetime. He desires a personal relationship with each one of us, yet He will not force His way into our hearts. He has given us the freedom to accept or reject His offer. And this invitation is not simply about acknowledging the work of the cross—it is about embracing *Rhema*, allowing God's living Word and power to enter your story and bring the transformation you were designed to experience.

"Whoever belongs to God hears what God says. The reason you do not hear is that you do not belong to God." John 8:47 (NIV)

This journey is unlike any other, because it requires surrender—the release of reliance on our own humanity and a wholehearted dependence on the faith-filled reality of the spiritual realm. Many books can inform, but only God's Word—empowered by the Holy Spirit—has the power to transform. Transformation is never about collecting facts; it is about walking in relationship with Jesus, hearing His voice, and being changed by His presence.

"For the word of God is alive and active. Sharper than any double-edged sword, it penetrates even to dividing soul and spirit, joints and marrow; it judges the thoughts and attitudes of the heart." (Hebrews 4:12 NIV).

The foundation of this journey is simple, yet profound: to know Him personally. From this place, every internal battle can be faced—and ultimately won. As we move forward, remember that victory does not begin with striving, but with abiding—leaning into the One who holds all the answers and has already won the ultimate battle within. Jesus said:

"Remain in me, as I also remain in you. No branch can bear fruit by itself; it must remain in the vine. Neither can you bear fruit unless you remain in me. I am the vine; you are the branches. If you remain in me and I in you, you will bear much fruit; apart from me you can do nothing." (John 15:4–5 NIV)

So, the question remains: *are you ready?*

Reflection Questions

1. Where in your life do you sense an unseen battle, and how do you usually respond—through your own strength or by relying on God?
2. What does it mean to you to move from simply knowing about Jesus (*oida*) to truly knowing Him (*ginōskō*)?
3. Which role of the Holy Spirit (Advocate, Comforter, Helper, Teacher, Guide, Protector) do you most need right now, and why?
4. How can you invite God's Word to move from information?
5. What step can you take this week to shift from striving to abiding in Jesus?

Prayer

Dear Jesus, I confess that I need You. I am a sinner, and my heart and mind depend on Your power, not my own. I long to know You more deeply through *ginōskō*—to truly experience You, not merely know about You. Let Your Word come alive and active within me. I do not want to rely on my own intellect or filter You through human ideas; I desire to know You personally.

Grant me Your power to change and to become all that You have called me to be. Prepare my heart for what You have planned and give me Your mind—the mind of Christ. In Jesus name - Amen!

Chapter 2
THREE-PART BEING: BODY, SOUL & SPIRIT

"May God himself, the God of peace, sanctify you through and through. May your whole spirit, soul and body be kept blameless at the coming of our Lord Jesus - 1 Thessalonians 5:23

Every human struggle—whether physical, emotional, or relational—is influenced by deeper spiritual realities. No lasting solution can be found apart from God, because spiritual problems cannot be resolved through physical or practical means alone. The roots of human brokenness reach back to the very beginning of time.

When Adam and Eve disobeyed God in the Garden, sin entered the world, followed swiftly by shame, fear, and separation from their Creator. Before Satan's deception, God had declared creation "very good" (Genesis 1:31). But after the fall, humanity became marked by dysfunction, hiding, blame-shifting, and generational brokenness.

What was lost in the Garden was reclaimed at the Cross. Through His death and resurrection, Jesus Christ reversed the curse and secured redemption for all who believe. In divine irony, God allowed Satan to participate in his own defeat—what the enemy intended for victory instead became the instrument of his downfall. The crucifixion became the pathway to salvation, healing, and reconciliation with the Father. From the Cross flowed forgiveness, grace, and mercy—restoring the broken relationship between God and mankind, and between humanity itself. In the end, the deceiver deceived himself, and the way was opened for humanity to be reconciled and restored to God's perfect purpose. This is where the opportunity to recover began.

Through Christ, we are offered not only eternal salvation but also freedom and wholeness in this present life. True freedom is not self-produced or circumstantial—it is the result of union with Christ, who alone has authority to release and sustain lasting freedom.

"So if the Son sets you free, you will be free indeed." —John 8:36 (NIV)

REDEMPTION IN OUR TIME

This truth is not just ancient history—it is our hope today. Families fracture under the weight of cultural shifts, economic pressures, and unresolved trauma. Generational wounds compound dysfunction, leaving homes vulnerable to the enemy's schemes.

Yet if the blood of Jesus is still enough—and Scripture assures us it is—then His redemption is as effective now as it was in Eden and at Calvary. The cross is timeless. Hope is still available, and healing is still possible.

GOD'S DESIGN: THREE-PART BEINGS

God created humanity as three-part beings—body, soul, and spirit. Each part is distinct yet inseparably connected. Because we are born spiritually dead, sin has affected every area of our being, leaving us vulnerable to deception and bondage. But there is hope!

"May God himself, the God of peace, sanctify you through and through. May your whole spirit, soul and body be kept

blameless at the coming of our Lord Jesus Christ."— 1 Thessalonians 5:23 (NIV)

True transformation is never partial. God does not heal one area and leave the rest broken; His desire is to restore us completely—body, soul, and spirit. Salvation is a divine act with immediate results, but the fullness of freedom requires intentional participation on our part.

Transformation unfolds over time as we nurture a deep, personal relationship with Jesus. The more time we spend in His presence, the more we are shaped into His likeness.

The Body

We must not confuse the body with the flesh. The body is our physical, non-eternal frame—the vessel that carries our soul and spirit and enables us to experience and engage with the world through our five senses. It includes the brain, nervous system, and all the systems essential for sustaining life. For all who have received His gift of life and choose to follow Him, the body becomes God's temple.

Before sin, Adam and Eve were immortal, sustained by God's presence. After the fall, their bodies, as well as all descendants that followed became subject to death, disease, and decay. The body, once a perfect dwelling of God's glory, became vulnerable to sickness, aging, and corruption.

The flesh is also one of the three primary enemies of the soul, alongside the world and Satan with his minions. By its very nature, it is sinful—constantly craving what is contrary to the Spirit—and therefore its desires must be resisted. Scripture makes it clear that the flesh will not be redeemed in this life; its redemption will come only when Jesus returns. Until then, we are called to deny the flesh, a task made possible only through spiritual maturity and the power of the Holy Spirit, who enables us to stand firm and walk in victory.

For the flesh desires what is contrary to the Spirit, and the Spirit what is contrary to the flesh." (Galatians 5:17)

"Those who live according to the flesh have their minds set on what the flesh desires…" (Romans 8:5–8)

The desires of the flesh must be denied, and only spiritual maturity, together with the presence and power of the Holy Spirit, can keep them held at bay. If we do not fully utilize everything Jesus has provided, the flesh will inevitably have its way.

"The acts of the flesh are obvious: sexual immorality, impurity and debauchery; idolatry and witchcraft; hatred, discord, jealousy, fits of rage, selfish ambition, dissensions, factions and envy; drunkenness, orgies, and the like. I warn you, as I did before, that those who live like this will not inherit the kingdom of God." (Galatians 5:19–21 NIV)

The following is a breakdown and simple explanation of the manifestations—the byproducts, or "fruits," of the flesh:

1. Sexual immorality
Greek: *porneia*
Any sexual activity outside God's design for covenant marriage between one man and one woman. Includes adultery, fornication, prostitution, pornography, and any misuse of sexuality. It is sex used for self, not as a holy gift within God's boundaries.

2. Impurity
Greek: *akatharsia* ("uncleanness")
Moral or sexual uncleanness in thought, motive, or behavior. Not just outward acts, but inner fantasies, twisted desires, or anything that pollutes the heart and mind. It's the opposite of purity and holiness.

3. Debauchery

Greek: *aselgeia* (often "sensuality" or "licentiousness")
Unrestrained, shameless living—no brakes. A lifestyle that says, "I'll do whatever I want," especially in sexual matters. It includes partying, perversion, and behavior with no regard for modesty or boundaries.

4. Idolatry

Greek: *eidōlolatria*
Worshiping anything instead of God—not just statues. It includes making an idol of money, success, a relationship, ministry, self, addiction, or anything we look to for identity, comfort, or security instead of the Lord.

5. Witchcraft

Greek: *pharmakeia* (from which we get "pharmacy")
Involvement in occult practices—sorcery, spells, rituals, contacting the dead, divination, tarot, astrology, curses, etc. In biblical context, it also connects to using substances, potions, or rituals to manipulate the spiritual realm. It is partnering with demonic power rather than the Holy Spirit.

6. Hatred

Deep hostility or ill-will toward others. A settled, inward attitude that wishes someone harm, holds malice, or refuses love. Hatred is the opposite of God's heart, who is love.

7. Discord

Greek: *eris* ("strife")
Stirring up conflict, arguing, and tension. This is the person who constantly creates drama, division, or tension through words, attitudes, or behavior. It's being quarrelsome instead of peace-making.

8. Jealousy
Greek: *zēlos* (can be good or bad; here it's bad)
A resentful desire for what someone else has—relationships, success, gifts, attention. It erodes gratitude and love and often leads to rivalry and comparison.

9. Fits of rage
Sudden outbursts of explosive anger—losing self-control, verbally or physically lashing out. It can involve yelling, threats, violence, or intimidating behavior. It is anger that is not surrendered to the Spirit.

10. Selfish ambition
Greek: *eritheia*
Self-centered drive that seeks personal advancement above others, even at their expense. It shows up as manipulation, political spirit, using people, or "me first" in ministry, family, or work. It's about building my kingdom, not God's.

11. Dissensions
Greek: *dichostasia* ("standing apart")
Deliberate division or rebellion against God's order or unity. This is when people stir up division, create "sides," or resist spiritual authority in unhealthy, fleshly ways. Tearing relationships or churches instead of seeking reconciliation.

12. Factions
Greek: *hairesis* (root of "heresy")
Click-forming, party spirit—creating exclusive groups that oppose others, often over opinions, doctrines, or loyalties. It includes sectarianism, elitism, or "us vs. them" attitudes inside the body of Christ.

13. Envy
Greek: *phthonos*

Not just wanting what others have but resenting that they have it. Envy can't rejoice in someone else's blessing, promotion, or favor. It corrodes love and joy.

14. Drunkenness

Habitual overuse of alcohol leading to loss of self-control. It dulls spiritual sensitivity, weakens judgment, and often opens the door to other sins. Scripture doesn't condemn all use of wine but clearly condemns being drunk (Ephesians 5:18).

15. Orgies

Greek: *kōmos*

Not just sexual orgies; the word also means wild carousing, unrestrained partying, nocturnal revelry often tied to pagan festivals, drunkenness, and immorality. It's "party life" that glorifies sin and excess.

16. "And the like"

Paul adds this phrase to show this is not a complete list. Anything that flows from the same spirit of the flesh—self-centered, rebellious against God, destructive to self and others—falls into the same category.

Although our flesh naturally gravitates toward unhealthy cravings and worldly desires, science reveals an extraordinary truth: the brain can be rewired through neuroplasticity. Neuroplasticity is the brain's remarkable ability to change, adapt, and reorganize throughout a person's life. It is often described as the brain's God-designed capacity to renew the mind, aligning beautifully with Romans 12:2.

Our brain is not fixed. It can change based on what we repeatedly do, think, and believe. It can learn, heal, create new pathways, and rewire old patterns based on what you think, feel, practice, and experience. Old thought patterns can be broken, and new pathways can be formed. As the Holy Spirit transforms us, what we learn and practice strengthens certain neural connections while weakening others, producing lasting behavioral change. This scientific reality beautifully reflects God's divine design for transformation—the renewing of the mind.

God's truth has the power to overwrite lies and dismantle old destructive programming, establishing new patterns aligned with His will. As we spend time with the Lord and come to *ginōskō*—know Him intimately—we are continually transformed into His likeness.

> *"Do you not know that your bodies are temples of the Holy Spirit...?" (1 Corinthians 6:19–20)*

> *"...offer your bodies as a living sacrifice, holy and pleasing to God..." (Romans 12:1)*

To cooperate with this process, we must understand a little about the nervous system:

- *Somatic nervous system* – governs voluntary actions, choices, and intentional movements.
- *Autonomic nervous system* – manages automatic functions like heartbeat, breath, and the stress response.

We have been clearly warned about the flesh and the need to keep it under control, denying its desires. Scripture teaches that our flesh—the sinful nature still connected to our physical body—remains corrupt until Christ's return. At salvation, our spirit is made alive, and our soul begins the ongoing process of renewal; yet our bodies continue to bear the effects of sin and mortality.

> *"We ourselves, who have the first fruits of the Spirit, groan inwardly as we wait eagerly for our adoption to sonship, the redemption of our bodies." - Romans 8:23 (NIV)*

This means that full redemption—including our physical bodies—will only be completed at the resurrection, when Jesus returns and transforms our mortal bodies into glorified ones. Until then, believers are called to deny the flesh (Romans 8:13; Galatians 5:16–17) and walk in the Spirit, allowing the Holy Spirit to empower us to overcome sinful desires and live in victory.

> *"For if you live according to the flesh, you will die; but if by the Spirit you put to death the misdeeds of the body, you will live." (Romans 8:13 NIV)*

> *"So I say, walk by the Spirit, and you will not gratify the desires of the flesh. For the flesh desires what is contrary to the Spirit, and the Spirit what is contrary to the flesh. They are in conflict with each other, so that you are not to do whatever you want." (Galatians 5:16–17 NIV)*

When trauma or sin programs our system, our bodies can remain "stuck" in fight, flight, or freeze. But Scripture assures us that discipline is possible, and thoughts can be filtered through truth and held captive before any action is taken.

> *"No, I strike a blow to my body and make it my slave so that after I have preached to others, I myself will not be disqualified for the prize." (1 Corinthians 9:27 NIV)*

> *"We demolish arguments and every pretension that sets itself up against the knowledge of God, and we take captive every thought to make it obedient to Christ." (2 Corinthians 10:5 NIV)*

The body plays a vital role in how we live out our faith. When surrendered to the Spirit, even our physical frame becomes an instrument of transformation, partnering with God to walk in true freedom. As Paul urges in Romans 12:1, we are to "offer our bodies as a living sacrifice, holy and pleasing to God—this is your true and proper worship." Likewise, in 1 Corinthians 6:19–20, we are reminded that our bodies are temples of the Holy Spirit, bought at a price, and therefore to be used for God's glory. In this way, the body is not just flesh and bone, but a vessel through which God's Spirit brings about freedom and transformation.

The Soul

After the fall in the garden, the soul became dominated by self rather than by the Holy Spirit. Instead of being Spirit-led, it became flesh-driven—subject to fear, shame, and confusion. The soul is the life within us: the decision-maker and the bridge between body and spirit. It encompasses the mind, will, and emotions, forming the seat of our personality and identity.

Within the soul, we interpret the world around us, make choices, form relationships, and develop internal patterns that ultimately shape how we live.

From birth, the soul begins absorbing input from family systems, culture, and personal experiences through the five senses. When a child grows up in an environment marked by anger, rejection, or chaos, those patterns become ingrained as "normal" and are often replayed in adulthood. Likewise, when culture continually bombards us with distorted messages about worth, identity, and success, the soul can internalize those lies until they feel true. Over time, the mind, will, and emotions become conditioned—sometimes by truth, but more often by distortion. This is why the soul is such a critical battleground: left unhealed, it fuels dysfunction; renewed by God's truth, it becomes the very foundation of freedom.

The soul functions much like the body's nervous system, operating with both voluntary and involuntary responses. God has given us free will, the ability to choose what we believe. Yet when those beliefs are unhealthy or rooted in deception, they inevitably influence how we think, feel, and act. While the decision to believe is voluntary, the resulting thoughts, emotions, and behaviors often become automatic and destructive, difficult to change until we return to and confront the original belief that produced them.

The Human Spirit

Before the fall, Adam and Eve's spirit was alive—in direct communion with God. When they disobeyed, their spirit died (Genesis 2:17). This does not mean they ceased to exist, but that they became spiritually disconnected from God, the Source of life. The spirit—the part of man designed for communion with God—lost its connection, light, and authority. From that moment, humanity became incapable of true fellowship with God apart from divine restoration through Jesus Christ.

The spirit is the God-breathed core of our being—the part created for direct relationship with Him. Without Christ, the spirit is dead, cut off from its source of life (Ephesians 2:1). At salvation, the spirit is made alive again, restored to fellowship with God, and given the ability to discern truth, resist deception, and walk in spiritual authority.

Even after the spirit is reborn, the soul and body often carry the residue of family dysfunction, cultural influence, and past programing. This creates inner tension—a renewed spirit longing for God's truth while the soul and body remain conditioned by old patterns of thinking and reacting. Spiritual maturity is the lifelong process of allowing the spirit—anchored in God's Word and empowered by the Holy Spirit—to lead, while the soul is renewed and the body brought into submission.

WHY INDIVIDUAL RE-PROGRAMMING MATTERS

Each part—body, soul, and spirit—carries the influence of what we've been exposed to. Family systems hand down patterns of communication, coping, and beliefs. Culture imposes narratives about identity, success, and morality. Trauma imprints survival strategies and thought patterns into our souls.

If we neglect any one part of our being, transformation remains incomplete:

- A healed spirit without renewed thoughts keeps us bound to old cycles.
- A renewed mind without caring for the body leaves us vulnerable to stress and dysregulation.
- A disciplined body without the Spirit's leadership can drift into pride or performance.

True freedom requires recognizing how each part—spirit, soul, and body—has been shaped by family patterns and cultural influences and then inviting God to redeem them all. The Spirit must lead, the soul must align with truth, and the body must come under God's design. Only then can we experience wholeness as He intended—free from the weight of inherited patterns and empowered to build a new legacy.

TRANSFORMING THE SOUL

Genesis 2:7 reveals that humanity became a living soul when God breathed His own life into the dust of the ground. The soul is not vague or mystical; it is the core of our inner life that expresses itself outwardly.

Scripture highlights the soul's dimensions:
- It worships: "My soul magnifies the Lord" (Luke 1:46).
- It struggles: "Now my soul is troubled" (John 12:27).
- It yearns: "My soul longs, yes, faints for the courts of the Lord" (Psalm 84:2).
- It endures beyond death (Matthew 10:28).

The soul is the battleground where truth and deception meet, making it both deeply valuable to God and fiercely challenged by the enemy.

THE THREE PARTS OF THE SOUL

Mind – The capacity to think, reason, and imagine. It is the place where previous experiences are stored—data shaped by memory, influenced by experience, and renewed by truth (Romans 12:2). What we have learned and lived through becomes the lens through which we interpret reality.

Will – The power of choice. Through the will, we either reject God's invitation or accept it—embracing His love and expressing our love for Him in return. The will functions as a gatekeeper, determining what we allow in and what we accept or reject before it takes root within us. It is here that we choose what to believe, and those beliefs, in turn, shape how we think, feel, and act moving forward.

Emotions – The capacity to feel deeply, shaping how we respond and act. Emotions add color and depth to life, yet they are designed to align with truth rather than deception (Psalm 42:5, NIV). When anchored in lies, emotions give rise to fear, shame, and despair; when grounded in truth, they produce joy, peace, and love—and directly influence our behavior. Together, these dimensions form the operating system of the soul.

THE PROGRAMMING OF THE SOUL

Like a computer that runs on code, the soul functions through programming and stored data. The will determines what is allowed in, the mind processes, interprets, and stores information, and the emotions translate that input into patterns of response. Over time, these interactions form beliefs and habits that shape how we live.

From birth, we begin absorbing information through our five senses. Family patterns, culture, and personal experiences feed the "data bank" of the soul. If truth is not intentionally planted, the default programming conforms to "the pattern of this world" (Romans 12:2). This explains why two people can face the same situation yet respond in completely different ways—their inner programming interprets reality through different lenses. The stored data within us determines whether we react or respond. In addition to this internal programming, there are two other sources of influence we must consider: demonic interference that seeks to distort truth and, for believers, the guiding presence of the Holy Spirit who leads us into all truth.

There are many potential contributors, but we will begin by addressing some of the more obvious surface issues before delving deeper into the underlying roots. Among the most common factors are generational curses and the breakdown of the family unit.

Generational Curses

Generational curses refer to patterns of sinful behavior, destructive habits, or spiritual strongholds that are passed down from one generation to the next. These cycles can manifest in various ways, such as addictions, unhealthy relationships, or negative mindsets, often continuing until they are confronted and broken through spiritual renewal and transformation.

"You shall not bow down to them or worship them; for I, the Lord your God, am a jealous God, punishing the children for the sin of the parents to the third and fourth generation of those who hate me." (Exodus 20:5)

However, it's also important to note that Scripture emphasizes personal responsibility and the ability to break free from these patterns of behavior.

"The son will not share the guilt of the father, nor will the father share the guilt of the son. The righteousness of the righteous will be credited to them, and the wickedness of the wicked will be charged against them." (Ezekiel 18:20)

This verse highlights that while generational influences exist, each person is accountable for their own choices. Through faith, renewing of the mind, and the power of the Holy Spirit, individuals can break free from destructive cycles and walk in the freedom and purpose God intends.

In a broader sense, generational curses can also be understood as the recurring patterns of dysfunction, behavior, and trauma that pass from one generation to the next. These cycles shape beliefs, responses, and relationships—often without conscious awareness. Breaking free from such patterns requires intentional recognition, a willingness to heal, and often the guidance of professional support through counseling, therapy, or spiritual mentorship.

A question frequently asked is whether the behaviors that pass from one generation to another can simply fade away on their own. Generational patterns often appear to skip a generation when behavior is interrupted without true inner transformation. One generation may avoid a particular sin externally, overcorrect through strict boundaries, or suppress behaviors without addressing the underlying heart issues. While outward conduct may change, unresolved roots remain. When the next generation lacks the same restraints, fear, or external structure, those hidden issues can resurface. The pattern did not disappear—it remained unhealed and vulnerable to spirit influence.

Similarly, there is an important distinction between environmental change and internal healing. A parent may escape addiction or abuse due to strong boundaries, physical distance, or enforced rules. However, if emotional wounds and trauma are not processed and healed, the next generation may inherit the internal impact. Without healthy coping mechanisms or spiritual and emotional integration, children often reenact the same root issues in different forms. Though the expression may change, the underlying cause remains the same.

Additionally, the breakdown of the family unit can be attributed to several complex and interrelated factors. Many families today face significant challenges that hinder emotional and spiritual health. Some of those major contributors include:

- *Parental Absence*—whether due to divorce, abandonment, or demanding work schedules, often leaves children with deep emotional wounds and unmet needs. Compounding this is a noticeable decline in moral and spiritual values, as society continues to drift from Biblical truth. This erosion has weakened the very foundation upon which strong families are built.
- *Cultural and societal influences*—such as individualism, secular ideologies, and media portrayals of broken homes have distorted the way relationships and family roles are perceived. At the same time, economic pressures, like financial hardship and job-related stress, place significant strain on marriages and parent-child dynamics.
- *Unresolved trauma*—whether rooted in past abuse, childhood pain, or generational patterns of dysfunction—often perpetuates cycles of brokenness. Only the healing power and presence of the Holy Spirit can truly restore what has been lost. As the Church, we are called to be agents of hope, healing, and truth, bringing restoration to families through the love of Christ and the guidance of the Holy Spirit.

Recognizing and understanding these contributing factors is an important step toward true restoration. Through awareness, faith, intentional healing, and the guidance of the Holy Spirit, individuals and families can break destructive cycles, overcome longstanding challenges, and experience genuine renewal. The following are some common contributing factors:

- *Monetary Pressures*—Financial strain can create tension and conflict within the family, disrupting emotional stability and unity.
- *Work / Family-Life Imbalance*—Demanding work schedules and long hours often reduce the quality and quantity of time spent together, weakening family connection and intimacy.
- *Breakdowns in Communication*—Poor communication and unresolved conflict foster emotional distance, misunderstanding, and resentment among family members.
- *Divorce and Separation*—The growing rate of divorce and separation disrupts family structure and can leave lasting emotional effects on both children and adults, impacting their sense of security and future relationships.
- *Substance Abuse*—Alcohol and drug addiction often lead to disconnect, neglect, abuse, and the erosion of trust, resulting in instability within the home.
- *Mental Health Challenges*—When mental health struggles are ignored or untreated, they can deeply affect relationships, disrupt family harmony, and in severe cases, lead to devastating loss.
- *Cultural Shifts*—Changing social values and moral standards have redefined traditional family roles, often creating confusion and instability in homes that lack firm spiritual grounding.
- *Media Distractions*—Excessive use of technology and social media diminishes meaningful face-to-face interaction, weakening emotional connection and family unity.
- *Inadequate Support Systems*—Without extended family, church, or community involvement, families often face hardship alone, increasing feelings of isolation and overwhelm.
- *Missing or Weak Spiritual Foundation*—Perhaps the most critical factor. Without God's presence and guidance, families are far more vulnerable to division and dysfunction. A strong spiritual foundation anchors the family in truth, shaping present relationships while influencing future generations with godly values, direction, and resilience.

Although every family is unique in its dynamics and experiences, the factors contributing to breakdown often share common threads. Healing and restoration require a combined effort—addressing issues at the individual level, within the family unit, and through the support of a caring community.

While these external factors are real, the deeper question remains: What is truly causing them? Before delving further, take a moment to reflect on your own personal experiences growing up.

There are also additional sources of input at work in our lives. As Spirit-led believers, the Holy Spirit gently speaks truth into our circumstances, offering wisdom, guidance, comfort, and peace. At the same time, demonic influence seeks to interfere—planting lies, stirring emotions, and provoking destructive reactions. This is why Scripture reminds us to be "quick to listen, slow to speak, and slow to become angry" (James 1:19, NIV), encouraging us to carefully discern and process each situation before taking action.

SYMPTOMS AND MANIFESTATIONS

When the soul is programmed through deception and dysfunction, the resulting fruit becomes evident in destructive behaviors (see Figure 1 & 2):

- Fear and anxiety
- Anger and rage
- Addictions and compulsions
- Shame and self-condemnation
- Control and manipulation
- Lust and immorality

These issues are not the root problem—they are symptoms, like bitter fruit growing from diseased soil. Addressing only behavior is like trimming branches while leaving the roots untouched. True healing occurs when the lies embedded in the

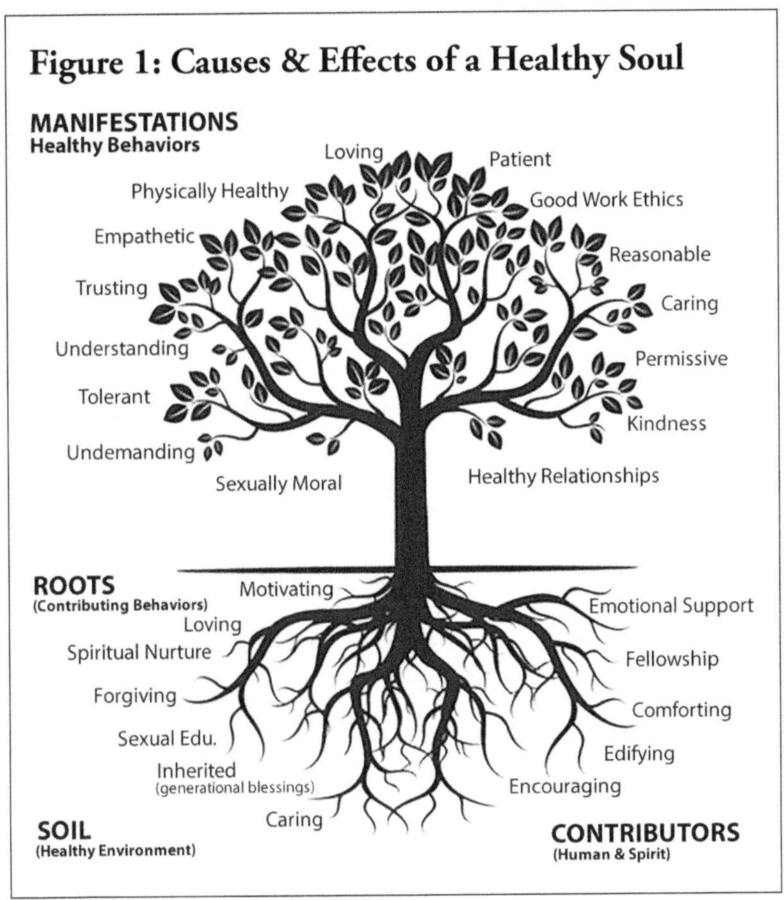

soul are exposed, uprooted, and replaced with God's truth. As the soul comes into alignment with the Spirit, new and healthy fruit begins to grow—"love, joy, peace, patience, kindness, goodness, faithfulness, gentleness, and self-control" (Galatians 5:22–23).

THE CYCLE OF CAUSE AND EFFECT

Every soul functions within a continuous cycle that either sustains freedom or perpetuates bondage. What we choose to believe shapes the way we think; the way we think determines how we feel; and how we feel ultimately influences the way we act.

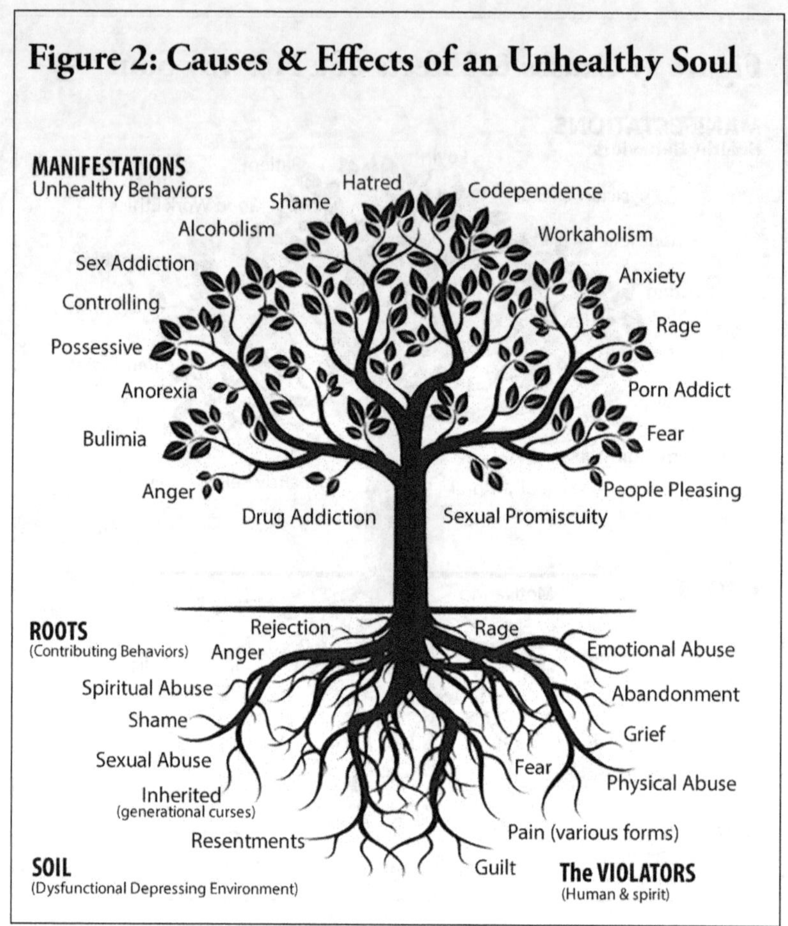

Beliefs —Thoughts —Feelings —Actions

- *Beliefs*—Are a matter of choice, rooted in our God-given free will. From our beliefs, the internal "operating system" of the soul begins to form. They serve as the foundation and root system upon which our lives are built.
- *Thoughts*—Emerge from those beliefs, shaping how we interpret life and producing corresponding feelings.

- *Feelings/Emotions*—Flow from our thoughts. The way we think determines how we feel. And how we feel influences how we act.
- *Actions*—Our behaviors are shaped by our emotions, and over time, these actions reinforce the original belief—whether rooted in truth or deception. This ongoing cycle produces either the fruits of the Spirit or the fruits of the deceiver, and it is through this process that strongholds are formed.

Because beliefs are the starting point, they carry the greatest weight. When beliefs are rooted in lies, they give rise to distorted thoughts, destructive emotions, and damaging behaviors. But when grounded in truth, they produce godly thoughts, healthy emotions, and life-giving behaviors that align with God's design.

BRINGING IT TOGETHER: THE INFORMATION INTERSECTION

Every thought and decision passes through an inner crossroads—the "information intersection"—where various inputs compete for influence and authority. As Scripture reminds us, "As a man thinks in his heart, so is he" (Proverbs 23:7). Our internal processing is never neutral; it actively shapes the direction and outcome of our lives (See Figures 3).

At this intersection, we get to choose what we accept and what we reject. These choices, up front, ultimately set the path toward either an irrational reaction or a healthy response:

- *Reaction* — impulsive, defensive, fear-driven, and flesh-led; it reinforces dysfunction.
- *Response* — Spirit-led and grounded in truth; it leads to growth and freedom.

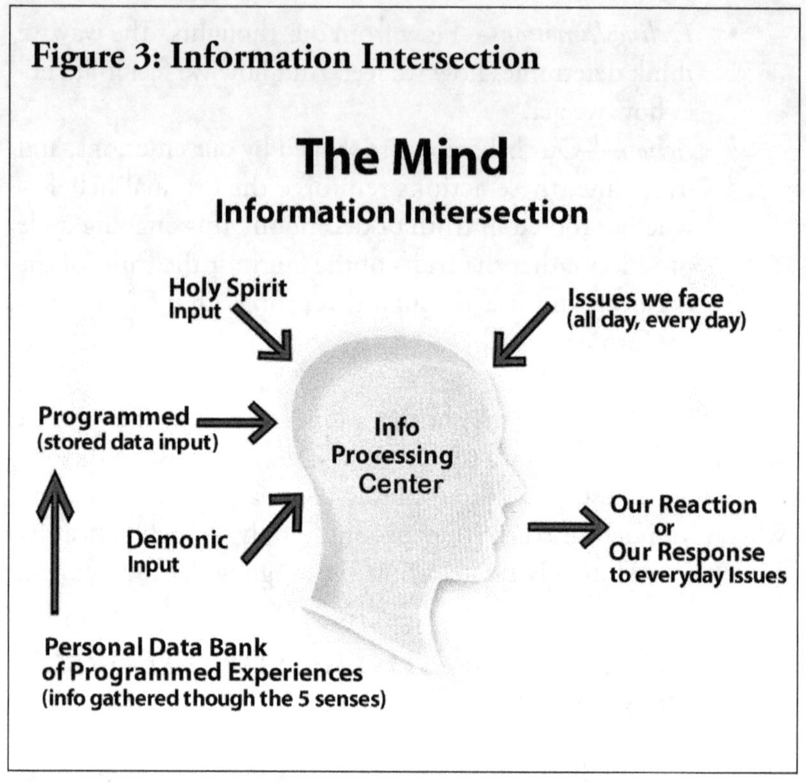

Being quick to listen and slow to speak, exercising wisdom in the moment, is vital because the outcome will directly reflect which input we choose to accept and act upon. As Scripture says:

> *"My dear brothers and sisters, take note of this: Everyone should be quick to listen, slow to speak and slow to become angry." (James 1:19, NIV)*

HOW PROCESSING WORKS

Every experience triggers a rapid yet consequential sequence within the soul:

- The mind recognizes an issue or provocation that needs to be addressed.
- It searches the internal "data bank" for the closest match based on past experiences.
- It evaluates the recalled information against the present situation.
- It then determines which influence to follow: the Holy Spirit, personal experience, or demonic suggestion. This sequence also shows up as ongoing self-talk. It runs constantly in the background—through every sight, sound, smell, taste, and touch—shaping our next move.
- We then move forward with what has been determined.

WHEN WOUNDS DISTORT PROPER PROCESSING

Without healing, unresolved pain skews the sequence:
- Past betrayal —produces suspicion even in safe relationships.
- Childhood neglect —abandonment feelings in ordinary conflict.
- Family/cultural systems —normalization of dysfunction instead of healthy confrontation.

AWARENESS: THE FIRST STEP TOWARDS CHANGE

Freedom begins with awareness—seeing life as it truly is, rather than through denial, distortion, or deception. Scripture urges:

"take every thought captive to make it obedient to Christ" (2 Corinthians 10:5).

Everything we allow into our lives must first be filtered through truth. It is the awareness and understanding of truth that exposes the lies we have believed and invites God's truth into the battleground of the soul. Denial keeps strongholds hidden, while awareness unmasks the enemy's schemes. When the light of truth shines on deception, the veil of denial is lifted, lies are exposed, and freedom becomes possible. Lasting change flows from aligning our minds with God's truth rather than conforming to worldly patterns.

> *"Do not conform to the pattern of this world, but be transformed by the renewing of your mind. Then you will be able to test and approve what God's will is—his good, pleasing and perfect will." Romans 12:2 (NIV)*

Through Christ, believers are never powerless. He has given us authority to bind what comes from the enemy and to loose what comes from God:

> *"I will give you the keys of the kingdom of heaven; whatever you bind on earth will be bound in heaven, and whatever you loose on earth will be loosed in heaven." (Matthew 16:19 NIV)*

This divine authority allows us to confront destructive programming at its root—through repentance, forgiveness, renunciation, and the renewing of the mind with God's truth.

Walking in this authority is a daily practice. It means continually aligning our thoughts, words, and actions with Scripture, resisting the enemy's lies, and inviting the Holy Spirit to lead every decision. As we do, freedom is not only received—it is maintained.

UNDERSTANDING THE HUMAN SPIRIT

The soul is not the only significant aspect of our inner world. At the core of our identity is the human spirit—the deepest part of who we are, created for relationship with God. When our human spirit is united with the Holy Spirit, we receive identity, authority, and power to walk in newness of life:

"Flesh gives birth to flesh, but the Spirit gives birth to spirit." (John 3:6 NIV)

"You are not controlled by the flesh but by the Spirit, if indeed the Spirit of God lives in you. Anyone who does not have the Spirit of Christ does not belong to Him. But if Christ is in you, even though the body is dead because of sin, the Spirit gives life because of righteousness. And if the Spirit of Him who raised Jesus from the dead lives in you, He who raised Christ will also give life to your mortal bodies through His Spirit who lives in you. Therefore, brothers and sisters, we have an obligation—but not to the flesh, to live according to it. For if you live according to the flesh, you will die; but if by the Spirit you put to death the misdeeds of the body, you will live. For all who are led by the Spirit of God are children of God." (Romans 8:9–14 NIV).

From this union flows the fruit of the Spirit—love, joy, peace, patience, kindness, goodness, faithfulness, gentleness, and self-control (Galatians 5:22–23).

The human spirit was created for intimate connection with the Holy Spirit. Without that divine connection, a God-shaped emptiness remains within us. The enemy seeks to exploit this vacuum, tempting us to fill it with substitutes—false comforts found in people, possessions, or pursuits—idols that can never truly satisfy. Because the need is spiritual, nothing natural can meet it; only God Himself can fill the inner void.

It is through the human spirit that we receive God's guidance, conviction, and continual renewal—restoring the fellowship that was fractured in the Garden (John 3:6). This divine union is both essential, profound and life-changing: the Holy Spirit indwells every true believer, joining Himself to our spirit so that we may walk according to the Spirit rather than the flesh.

Paul explains that through Christ, the law of the Spirit who gives life has set us free from the law of sin and death. What the Law couldn't accomplish—because human flesh is weak—God did by sending His own Son in human likeness as a sin offering, and in Jesus' body He condemned sin.

> *"I will give you a new heart and put a new spirit in you; I will remove from you your heart of stone and give you a heart of flesh. And I will put my Spirit in you and move you to follow my decrees and be careful to keep my laws." (Ezekiel 36:26–27 NIV)*

> *"Therefore, there is now no condemnation for those who are in Christ Jesus, because through Christ Jesus the law of the Spirit who gives life has set you free from the law of sin and death. For what the law was powerless to do because it was weakened by the flesh, God did by sending his own Son in the likeness of sinful flesh to be a sin offering. And so he condemned sin in the flesh, in order that the righteous requirement of the law might be fully met in us, who do not live according to the flesh but according to the Spirit. Those who live according to the flesh have their minds set on what the flesh desires; but those who live in accordance with the Spirit have their minds set on what the Spirit desires. The mind governed by the flesh is death, but the mind governed by the Spirit is life and peace." (Romans 8:1–6 NIV).*

Immediate and enduring blessings that flow from the union of our spirit with the Holy Spirit include:

He dwells within

God no longer dwells in temples made by human hands—He dwells within His people, making every believer a living dwelling place of His presence sanctifying and transforming us from the inside out:

> *"Do you not know that your bodies are temples of the Holy Spirit, who is in you, whom you have received from God? You are not your own;" 1Corinthians 6:19 (NIV)*

> *"And we all, who with unveiled faces contemplate the Lord's glory, are being transformed into his image with ever-increasing glory, which comes from the Lord, who is the Spirit." 2 Corinthians 3:18 (NIV)*

He provides spiritual wisdom and direction

Jesus promises that the Holy Spirit would continue His ministry—teaching, reminding, and guiding believers into truth long after His physical departure.

> *"But the Advocate, the Holy Spirit, whom the Father will send in my name, will teach you all things and will remind you of everything I have said to you." (John 14:26 NIV)*

> *"But when he, the Spirit of truth, comes, he will guide you into all the truth. He will not speak on his own; he will speak only what he hears, and he will tell you what is yet to come." John 16:13 (NIV)*

He empowers

Giving strength, courage, and resilience to overcome sin and trial, Paul's prayer emphasizes that true strength comes from the

Holy Spirit working within, empowering believers at the deepest level of their inner life.

> *"I pray that out of his glorious riches he may strengthen you with power through his Spirit in your inner being,"* *(Ephesians 3:16 NIV)*

> *"But you will receive power when the Holy Spirit comes on you; and you will be my witnesses in Jerusalem, and in all Judea and Samaria, and to the ends of the earth."* *(Acts 1:8 NIV)*

He transforms

Renewing our inner life, restoring peace and joy, while changing us into the likeness of Christ. These qualities are not produced by effort but by abiding in the Spirit—evidence of inner transformation rather than external rule-keeping.

> *"May the God of hope fill you with all joy and peace as you trust in him, so that you may overflow with hope by the power of the Holy Spirit." (Romans 15:13 NIV)*

> *"But the fruit of the Spirit is love, joy, peace, forbearance, kindness, goodness, faithfulness, gentleness and self-control. Against such things there is no law." (Galatians 5:22–23 NIV)*

He desires relationship

Drawing us into intimate fellowship with the Father and the Son. Life in the Spirit replaces fear with sonship, as the Holy Spirit assures believers of their true identity and deep intimacy with the Father. This is the life of the Trinity made personal to us: grace through Christ, love from the Father, and ongoing fellowship with the Holy Spirit.

> *"The Spirit you received does not make you slaves, so that you live in fear again; rather, the Spirit you received brought about your adoption to sonship. And by him we cry,*

> *'Abba, Father.' The Spirit himself testifies with our spirit that we are God's children." (Romans 8:15–16 NIV)*

> *"May the grace of the Lord Jesus Christ, and the love of God, and the fellowship of the Holy Spirit be with you all." (2 Corinthians 13:14 NIV)*

GOD'S PROMISE OF RENEWAL

God Himself promises to restore what sin has broken:

> *"I will give you a new heart and put a new spirit in you; I will remove from you your heart of stone and give you a heart of flesh. And I will put my Spirit in you and move you to follow my decrees and be careful to keep my laws." Ezekiel 36:26–27 (NIV)*

And when our earthly life comes to an end, Scripture reminds us of an eternal reality: though the body passes away, the soul and spirit continue into eternity with Christ—fully restored and forever united with Him.

> *"...the dust returns to the ground it came from, and the spirit returns to God who gave it." (Ecclesiastes 12:7 NIV)*

As the Holy Spirit illuminates God's Word (*rhema*), He interacts with our spirit to bring about genuine transformation. Regeneration is God's gift, but deep and lasting change develops over time as we intentionally pursue His presence. The more time we spend with Jesus, the more His character is formed within us, and the more we reflect His likeness:

> *"And we all, who with unveiled faces contemplate the Lord's glory, are being transformed into his image with ever-increasing glory, which comes from the Lord, who is the Spirit." (2 Corinthians 3:18 NIV)*

UNDERSTANDING THE HUMAN HEART

Before moving deeper, it helps to distinguish between the spirit, the soul, and the heart. Scripture sometimes uses these terms interchangeably, but there is a helpful nuance to see their distinct roles:

- The spirit is our direct connection to God's Spirit, the part of us that is reborn at salvation and designed for communion with Him.
- The soul is the seat of the mind, will, and emotions—the ground control of our being, where we consciously process life, interpret experiences, and make decisions.
- The heart is the inner core of motives, desires, and intentions—the wellspring that directs the soul and reveals what and who we truly love.

Human Heart and Soul Working Together

The heart determines what we believe and love, and the soul expresses those beliefs through thought, emotion, and choice—when the heart is healed, the soul is restored.

The prophet Jeremiah gives a sobering picture:

"The heart is deceitful above all things and beyond cure. Who can understand it?" — Jeremiah 17:9

God alone discerns and heals the heart. His Word penetrates to its deepest places with surgical precision:

"For the word of God is alive and active. Sharper than any double-edged sword, it penetrates even to dividing soul and spirit, joints and marrow; it judges the thoughts and attitudes of the heart." —Hebrews 4:12

At salvation, God initiates the immediate miracle of transformation. He removes the hardened heart of stone and replaces it with a heart of flesh. He places His Spirit within us, empowering us to walk in obedience and reshaping our desires and motives.

"I will give you a new heart and put a new spirit in you; I will remove from you your heart of stone and give you a heart of flesh. And I will put my Spirit in you and move you to follow my decrees and be careful to keep my laws. (Ezekiel 36:26–27 NIV)

Yet transformation, unlike salvation, is not instantaneous; it unfolds as we intentionally spend time with Him, surrendering our will, intentions, and even our hidden motives to Him. This daily surrender is the life Jesus described when He said:

"Whoever wants to be my disciple must deny themselves and take up their cross daily and follow me" (Luke 9:23 NIV).

The soul may process information, but the heart directs its course. Until the heart is fully surrendered, the soul cannot flourish in truth. Yet when God renews the heart, the soul comes into alignment with His will, and the whole person begins to reflect His glory. This heart renewal paves the way for the renewing of the mind, where old patterns, strongholds are replaced with truth, and transformation becomes both internal and lasting.

Reflection Questions:
Where do you see evidence of faulty programming in your thoughts or behaviors?

1. Which part of your soul (mind, will, emotions) needs to surrender to the Spirit right now?
2. What strongholds—lies you've treated as truth—might God be calling you to confront with His Word?
3. How do your daily choices reflect alignment with either the Kingdom of Light or the kingdom of darkness?

What practices could you adopt this week to renew your mind and invite the Holy Spirit to reshape your inner programming (Scripture meditation, confession/renunciation, prayer, fasting, community accountability)?

Closing Prayer
Father, search my heart and reveal where my soul has been shaped by lies rather than truth. Expose every stronghold that holds me captive and shine the light of Your Word into every hidden place. Renew my mind, heal my emotions, and strengthen my will to choose You each day. Bring my body, soul, and spirit into alignment under Your lordship, and empower me to walk in lasting freedom and wholeness through the power of the Holy Spirit. In Jesus' name, Amen.

Chapter 3
FRAGMENTATION OF THE SOUL

"He restores my soul. He guides me in paths of righteousness for His name's sake." — Psalm 23:3"

The soul is not only shaped by sin and false beliefs; at times its injuries run far deeper. While lies often serve as the doorway, some wounds are so profound that they fracture the soul itself. This kind of pain goes beyond surface-level thoughts and emotions, leaving an imprint on the brain, the soul, and even touching the spirit. The result can be profound confusion, with a person feeling as though restoration is out of reach.

The world often describes this condition as trauma that leads to dissociation or, in more severe cases, Dissociative Identity Disorder (formerly known as multiple personality disorder), typically identified through clinical diagnosis. While this discussion will not explore the medical or technical dimensions in depth, it is important to acknowledge their legitimacy and complexity.

Profound soul fragmentation frequently requires a holistic response—a partnership between appropriate professional intervention and deep, compassionate spiritual care. In many respects, the capacity to dissociate can be understood as a protective grace, allowing a child—or even an adult—to survive overwhelming and unbearable circumstances when no other form of help is available. This divinely permitted survival mechanism sustains the individual until the opportunity for genuine healing and restoration emerges.

THE ORPHAN SPIRIT AND FRAGMENTATION

The orphan spirit is often described as a condition affecting a person's inner life—especially their sense of identity, belonging, and security. It is not widely understood and is rarely discussed, yet its effects can be profound.

The "orphan spirit" is best understood as operating primarily in the soul—the mind, will, and emotions—where wounds, beliefs, and identity narratives are formed. It is deep-seated feelings of abandonment, rejection and emotional distance from others. It constantly tells the person they have been rejected, are not good enough, insignificant, alienated, and isolated. They can even struggle comprehending God's love for them.

Even after a person is born again and the Holy Spirit dwells within them, an orphan mindset can remain in the soul with self-talk whispering, "I don't measure up, I'm on my own, I must earn love, I don't belong." This is why transformation is not merely an event but a process: God not only saves the spirit, He restores the soul and renews the mind. As the heart is healed and the mind renewed, the Holy Spirit replaces fear with sonship, striving with security, and counterfeit comfort with true communion—until what is true in our spirit becomes established in our inner life and begins to manifest as real change from within.

There are husbands and wives who share a home, raise children, sleep in the same bed, and build an entire life together—yet their souls have never truly connected. Their bodies are present, but their hearts remain guarded and distant. This is one of the quiet tragedies of the orphan spirit: it allows people to look connected on the outside while living disconnected on the inside.

Many men struggle to give themselves fully to their wives because of unaddressed trauma and unresolved wounds. They become providers—busy, distracted, and responsible—physically present but emotionally unavailable. This type of marriage can slowly drift into a roommate dynamic, where deeper connection is avoided and intimacy becomes rare or reduced to a physical function. They are roommates with benefits, lacking a deep secure loving heart connection.

Many women can keep a beautiful home, nurture their families, maintain routines, and meet every outward expectation, yet still feel unappreciated, disconnected, unworthy, unwanted or unseen. They may appear strong and composed, but internally they feel orphaned—functioning on the outside while longing to be known, valued, and securely loved on the inside.

The orphan spirit makes healthy love feel unsafe, distorting affection and turning tenderness into a perceived threat. It convinces the heart that love is temporary, keeping a person guarded, striving, and unable to fully receive the security God intends.

CODEPENDENT BEHAVIOR AND FRAGMENTATION

Codependent behavior is a form of counterfeit comfort, often closely connected to soul fragmentation. In many cases, both emerge from fragmentation and continue to reinforce one another over time. Soul fragmentation occurs when parts of the soul—the mind, will, and emotions—begin to divide internally as a survival response to pain, fear, abandonment, trauma, or unsafe attachment, often rooted in early life experiences. Codependency frequently develops within these same conditions. Instead of finding security and resting in God's safety, the soul learns to remain on high alert—constantly monitoring others' moods, needs, and approval in an effort to fit in, gain acceptance, and feel secure. In this way, comfort is sought from a counterfeit source rather than from the True Comforter—the Holy Spirit—

who dwells within every genuine believer.

Over time, this pattern pulls the heart away from trusting God and places emotional dependence on people. What began as protection slowly becomes exhaustion. God never asked you to carry the emotional weight of others. He invites you into peace, not pressure.

"Cast all your anxiety on him because he cares for you."
1 Peter 5:7 (NIV)

When we live in constant fear of rejection or abandonment, our nervous system remains on high alert. Yet Scripture reminds us that our security is not found in people, but in God's faithful presence alone.

"You will keep in perfect peace those whose minds are stead-
fast, because they trust in you." Isaiah 26:3 (NIV)

True healing begins when the soul learns it is safe again—not because people behave perfectly, but because God is trustworthy.

"The Lord is close to the brokenhearted and saves those who
are crushed in spirit."Psalms 34:18 (NIV)

Through Christ, we are invited out of striving and into rest—out of emotional survival and into spiritual security.

"Come to me, all you who are weary and burdened, and I
will give you rest." Matthew 11:28 (NIV)

Codependency is not a character flaw—it is often a learned response to pain. God does not shame survival strategies; He gently heals them. As truth replaces fear and relationship replaces performance, the soul begins to rest again.

"Then you will know the truth, and the truth will set you free." John 8:32 (NIV)

Healing cannot come through willpower alone. Old survival systems cannot contain resurrection life. This journey is not about fixing yourself—it is about allowing God to make you new. When the heart is renewed, the soul can finally rest in Christ.

"If anyone is in Christ, the new creation has come: The old has gone, the new is here!" (2 Corinthians 5:17, NIV)

ADDICTIVE BEHAVIOR AND FRAGMENTATION

Addictive behavior is both a result of soul fragmentation and a pattern that deepens it over time. The two are closely connected and often reinforce one another in a repeating cycle. Addiction typically forms when a person discovers something that temporarily soothes an unbearable internal state. In trauma-informed terms, addiction often functions as a protector part—its goal is simply to make the pain stop. However, because it offers relief without true healing, dependency gradually develops. Over time, this addictive part can become dominant, while other aspects of the soul are increasingly suppressed. This would be considered a form of idolatry, a counterfeit comfort as well.

True healing in these areas depends not only on therapeutic or clinical support but, most importantly, on the power of the Holy Spirit, the true Comforter. The human spirit—made alive in Christ—plays an active role in the restoration process. As the Holy Spirit partners with the human spirit, fractured aspects of the soul can be healed and integrated. What remains impossible through human effort alone becomes possible through God's grace.

"He heals the brokenhearted and binds up their wounds."
—Psalm 147:3

WHAT IS SOUL CARE?

Soul care is the intentional process of tending to the wounds that have shaped our operating system. Much of this internal programming was formed during seasons of life when we had little or no control—through childhood experiences, traumatic events, or environments that shaped us in ways we did not choose. These moments leave deep impressions within the soul, quietly influencing our thoughts, emotions, and behaviors—like an unseen operating system running in the background.

Because of this, much of our programming operates beneath the surface, quietly influencing how we think, feel, and act—often without our awareness. God does not punish us for being wounded; instead, He lovingly invites us into healing. He knows the soul has been damaged by the brokenness of this world and offers restoration to all who seek Him.

True healing addresses the condition of fragmentation—where the mind, will, and emotions have been fractured by trauma, false beliefs, or spiritual intrusion. Soul care is the process of cooperating with the Holy Spirit as He exposes corrupted inner programming and leads us toward wholeness, integration, and peace.

WHAT IS A FRAGMENTED SOUL?

Scripture teaches that we are made up of body, soul, and spirit (1 Thessalonians 5:23). When the soul (our inner life) is wounded—through abuse, loss, fear, betrayal, or sin—it can become "broken" or "fragmented."

Simply put, a fragmented soul is a soul that has been broken into parts, with some portions hidden or buried. This fragmentation can result in emotional instability, identity confusion, memory gaps, and difficulty forming healthy connections with both God and others. Left unaddressed, it traps individuals in cycles of dysfunction and hinders them from fully living out their identity in Christ.

But fragmentation is not the end of the story. Soul care provides a path toward restoration—bringing hidden wounds into the light, replacing lies with God's truth, and gathering the scattered pieces of the soul into unity under His Lordship.

The God who first breathed life into humanity is the same God who restores and redeems every fractured place within us. Where trauma divides, He unites. Where lies scatter, He gathers.

Where shame silences, He speaks truth. Healing the fragmented soul is not about erasing the past but about reclaiming wholeness through Christ, who came to heal the brokenhearted and bind up their wounds (Isaiah 61:1; Psalm 147:3).

BIBLICAL TRUTH ABOUT FRAGMENTATION

Scripture clearly acknowledges the reality of a divided inner life and its consequences. James describes this condition plainly, highlighting the inner conflict that arises when the soul is fractured.

"Such a person is double-minded and unstable in all they do"
(James 1:8, NIV)

The Psalms vividly portray the destructive nature of such fragmentation. David cries out, describing an inner life under attack and pulled apart.

"Or they will tear me apart like a lion and rip me to pieces with no one to rescue me" (Psalms 7:2, NIV)

In contrast, God's redemptive response is revealed in Psalm 23: The phrase "He refreshes my soul" carries the idea of restoring, gathering, and healing what has been torn.

"He refreshes my soul. He guides me along the right paths for his name's sake" (Psalms 23:3, NIV).

Jesus affirms this restorative mission in His own words. Quoting Isaiah, He declares that He was sent "to heal the brokenhearted"—to mend what has been shattered within.

"The Spirit of the Lord is on me, because he has anointed me to proclaim good news to the poor. He has sent me to proclaim freedom for the prisoners and recovery of sight for the blind, to set the oppressed free" (Luke 4:18 NIV)

HOW FRAGMENTATION HAPPENS

A fragmented soul happens when a person's inner being—mind, will, and emotions—has become divided, disconnected, or "fractured" due to trauma, sin, deep emotional pain, or prolonged spiritual conflict. In essence, a fragmented soul is a divided self—where parts of one's inner world (such as trust, peace, or identity) have been suppressed or trapped in past pain. In psychology, this is sometimes understood as dissociation—a coping mechanism where the mind separates itself from overwhelming experiences to protect the person from emotional overload.

Fragmentation does not happen in a vacuum; it develops as life's pressures, wounds, and spiritual battles collide with our inner world. Each cause—whether trauma, sin, oppression, or unhealthy attachment—chips away at the wholeness God intended. Over time, these breaks accumulate and begin to influence how we see ourselves, relate to others, and even how we perceive God. Left unhealed, fragmentation leaves us living fractured lives—functioning outwardly but feeling divided within.

Common Signs of Fragmentation

- *Feeling emotionally stuck in a past version of oneself.* Parts of the soul remain trapped in earlier seasons of pain, unable to grow beyond what happened.
- *Swinging between extreme states without clear cause.* Mood and identity can shift dramatically, revealing instability at the core.
- *Dissociation or memory gaps.* Whole sections of time may be missing, reflecting the mind's attempt to shield itself from trauma.
- *Overreactions to present situations triggered by past pain.* Current events stir disproportionate emotions because unresolved wounds are still active beneath the surface.
- *Sudden shifts in identity*—confident one day, insecure the next. The fractured soul struggles to find stability, moving between opposing self-perceptions.
- *Difficulty maintaining relationships or spiritual grounding.* Bonds with others, and even connection with God, are disrupted by unresolved inner divisions.
-

At the core is ongoing inner conflict and cycles of self-sabotage. A fragmented soul cannot find lasting peace until the broken places are addressed and healed. Recognizing these patterns is often the first step toward restoration, because Jesus longs to bring wholeness to every broken place.

> *"May your whole spirit, soul, and body be preserved blameless" (1 Thessalonians 5:23).*

True restoration of the fragmented soul begins with the presence and ministry of the Holy Spirit. While counseling and therapeutic care help uncover and process the layers of pain, only God's Spirit can reach the innermost places of the human heart where the damage resides. The Holy Spirit gently exposes the fractures caused by trauma, inviting truth into places long ruled by fear, shame, and survival mechanisms.

Healing occurs as the Holy Spirit reunites what was divided, restoring connection between the wounded parts of the soul and bringing them under the lordship of Christ. This is not a process of erasing parts of one's identity, but rather reclaiming what was lost—integrating the fragmented self into wholeness, peace, and alignment with God's design. Jesus declared His mission clearly:

> *"He has sent Me to heal the brokenhearted, to proclaim liberty to the captives and recovery of sight to the blind, to set at liberty those who are oppressed" (Luke 4:18, NKJV).*

Through His Spirit, that same ministry continues today. Where trauma once shattered identity, the Spirit of Truth brings clarity, stability, and renewal. What once operated in chaos can now come into order. What once hid in darkness can be gently brought into the light. Over time, as trust in God deepens, the person begins to experience internal peace—no longer surviving, but truly living as one whole, restored creation.

Steps Toward Healing

1. Invite the Holy Spirit to Identify Fractures

Healing begins with humility and openness. Ask the Spirit to reveal memories, inner vows, or patterns tied to fragmentation—moments of trauma, fear, or lies believed in vulnerable seasons. This often works best alongside a counselor or trusted inner-healing process.

2. Renounce Lies and Ungodly Agreements

Lies such as "I'm unlovable," "I'm beyond repair," or "I can't do anything right" are destructive agreements that shape how we see ourselves, others, and even God. Over time, they become strongholds that trap us in shame and defeat. God has given His

Word as a weapon to demolish lies. Every false belief must be broken and replaced with truth so that our minds are renewed and our identity restored.

> *"Do not conform to the pattern of this world, but be transformed by the renewing of your mind. Then you will be able to test and approve what God's will is—His good, pleasing and perfect will." (Romans 12:2 NIV)*

Common lies and God's truth:

Lie: "I am unlovable."
Truth: "I have loved you with an everlasting love; therefore with lovingkindness have I drawn you." (Jeremiah 31:3)

Lie: "I will never change."
Truth: "If anyone is in Christ, he is a new creation… all things have become new."(2 Corinthians 5:17)

Lie: "I'm beyond repair."
Truth: "He heals the brokenhearted and binds up their wounds." (Psalm 147:3)

Lie: "I can't do anything right."
Truth: "I can do all things through Christ which strengtheneth me." (Philippians 4:13, KJV)

Lie: "God has abandoned me."
Truth: "I will never leave you nor forsake you." (Hebrews 13:5)

Lie: "My past defines me."
Truth: "There is therefore now no condemnation to them which are in Christ Jesus."(Romans 8:1)

Breaking lies is not only rejecting falsehood; it is planting God's Word until truth becomes louder than the lie. Transformation begins as His promises rewrite the story of our lives.

3. Break Soul Ties and Ungodly Attachments

Severing unhealthy emotional or spiritual attachments is a crucial step. These ties—often called soul ties—form through sin, trauma, manipulation, or unhealthy dependency.

Instead of life-giving connection, they entangle the soul and keep it fragmented, binding us to people, places, or experiences that no longer align with God's design.

Such bonds can feel powerful because they are fueled by deep emotion, unmet needs, or even spiritual oppression. They may surface as obsessive thoughts, unhealthy longings, or cycles of guilt and shame. Left unbroken, they scatter the heart.

In Christ, freedom is possible. In prayer, name the attachment, renounce it, and break agreement with it in Jesus' name. As we release what bound us, the Holy Spirit gathers the fragments and restores wholeness. This is rarely a one-time event; it is a journey of recognizing, naming, and releasing as the Holy Spirit reveals.

4. Gather Back the Fragments

Through prayer, invite Jesus to gather and restore every fractured part of your being—mind, will, and emotions—bringing them into alignment under His Lordship. Trauma, sin, betrayal, and painful experiences can scatter us internally, leaving pieces of identity stuck in the past or held captive by fear and shame. Only Jesus can call back what has been lost, integrate what has been broken, and re-establish His peace in the deepest places of the soul.

As we surrender each area of fragmentation, our inner world comes into order under His authority—no longer ruled by fear, shame, or survival responses, but by the Spirit of truth and the love of God. This practice of prayerful surrender is an ongoing rhythm.

Prayer:

"Lord, please gather the scattered pieces of my heart. Bring my mind into clarity, my will into obedience, and my emotions into peace under Your authority. In Jesus name I pray, Amen"

5. Let Jesus Heal the Wounds

Healing is not merely a moment; it is a process. God can bring breakthrough in an instant, yet most often healing unfolds as we continue to walk with Him. This journey requires ongoing intimacy with Christ, consistent exposure to His Word, and the humility to receive help through the body of Christ. Wise believers, pastoral counselors, and trained ministers become instruments of His care.

As Jesus restores the soul, evidence emerges: confusion gives way to clarity, chaos to peace, aimlessness to purpose. Step by step, the fractured parts of life come into order under His authority. Healing is both gift and journey—God's grace restoring what was broken and our choice to keep walking with Him as He completes the work.

Prayer:

Father God, "I ask for Your help in leading me where I need to go. The idea of a fragmented soul and the faulty programming of my soul can feel overwhelming. Take me where I need to go. Where my soul has been fragmented, heal and restore me. Where I have believed lies, replace them with Your truth. Where ungodly attachments have bound me, break every chain in Jesus' name. Gather back every scattered piece of my heart and align my mind, will, and emotions under Your Lordship. Fill me with Your Spirit, that I may walk in wholeness, freedom, and peace. In Jesus' name, Amen."

Chapter 4
THE INVISIBLE CONFLICT

"Our struggle is not against flesh and blood, but against the rulers, against the authorities, against the powers of this dark world and against the spiritual forces of evil in the heavenly realms." —Ephesians 6:12

Scripture reveals that creation is not limited to what we can see. Alongside the physical world exists a vast and complex spiritual realm created by God and governed by His authority. Within this unseen order are spiritual beings—some loyal to God and serving His purposes, and others who rebelled against Him and now oppose His work. The Bible does not present this realm as mythology or speculation but as a real dimension of creation that interacts with human history. To understand the spiritual conflict described throughout Scripture, we must first recognize how this rebellion began and how it continues to influence the world today. The Bible makes it clear that the visible world is not all there is. Beyond what we can see lies an unseen realm—a spiritual conflict that predates humanity itself. At the center of this cosmic struggle is the rebellion and fall of Satan, setting in motion a war that continues to influence the course of humanity.

THE ORIGINAL CONFLICT

Originally created as a magnificent angel, Lucifer—whose name means morning star—was adorned with beauty and entrusted with great authority in God's presence (Ezekiel 28:12–15). Yet pride took root in his heart. Rather than worshiping God, he sought to exalt himself above God's throne:

> *"You said in your heart, 'I will ascend to the heavens; I will raise my throne above the stars of God… I will make myself like the Most High. But you are brought down to the realm of the dead, to the depths of the pit."*—Isaiah 14:13–15

In his rebellion, Satan led a host of angels astray. Revelation describes this cosmic revolt:

> *"The great dragon was hurled down—that ancient serpent called the devil, or Satan, who leads the whole world astray. He was hurled to the earth, and his angels with him."*— Revelation 12:9

These fallen angels became what we now know as demons— spiritual beings devoted to opposing God's purposes and corrupting His creation. What began as pride in heaven became an unending war against all that is good, holy, and true.

THE ONGOING INVISIBLE WAR

Since that moment, all of human history has unfolded against the backdrop of this unseen conflict. While angels continue to serve God and minister to His people, demons work tirelessly to deceive, tempt, and destroy. Both are spiritual beings, yet their nature and purpose could not be more opposite—one devoted to advancing God's Kingdom, the other determined to oppose it.

This is why Paul reminds us:

"Our struggle is not against flesh and blood, but against the rulers, against the authorities, against the powers of this dark world and against the spiritual forces of evil in the heavenly realms." —Ephesians 6:12

To walk faithfully, believers must learn to discern this realm—not to obsess over it, but to recognize how it shapes our reality and to live in the confidence that Christ has already triumphed over it.

ANGELS: GOD'S MESSENGERS AND SERVANTS

The word angel comes from the Greek *angelos*, meaning "messenger." Angels are created spiritual beings who serve God and carry out His will. They are powerful and purposeful agents of God's Kingdom. Their existence is everlasting from the point of creation forward, but they do not share God's eternal nature. Angels are created, immortal, and eternal in the sense of having no end, but not in the sense of having no beginning.

"They can no longer die; for they are like the angels." —Luke 20:36 (NIV)

Scripture highlights several truths about angels:

- *Created by God* – "For in Him all things were created: things in heaven and on earth, visible and invisible, whether thrones or powers or rulers or authorities; all things have been created through Him and for Him." (Colossians 1:16)
- *Powerful, but not all-powerful* – "Praise the LORD, you His angels, you mighty ones who do His bidding, who obey His word." (Psalm 103:20)

- *Organized by rank and role* – Seraphim, cherubim, and archangels serve distinct functions in God's order (Isaiah 6:2; Jude 1:9).
- *Do not marry or reproduce* – "At the resurrection people will neither marry nor be given in marriage; they will be like the angels in heaven." (Matthew 22:30)
- *Sent to protect and minister* – "Are not all angels ministering spirits sent to serve those who will inherit salvation?" (Hebrews 1:14; cf. Psalm 91:11).

Some angels are named in Scripture, and their roles reveal rank and authority much like generals in an army:
- Gabriel announced the birth of Jesus to Mary (Luke 1:30–38).
- Michael, the archangel, battles demonic forces in Daniel 10:13 and leads heaven's armies against Satan in Revelation 12:7–9.

Angels are loyal servants of God, wholly devoted to carrying out His will. They are not to be worshiped (Revelation 19:10), but they are to be acknowledged as integral agents in God's divine order—ministering to believers, protecting God's people, and fulfilling His purposes in the unseen realm.

> *"At this I fell at his feet to worship him. But he said to me, 'Don't do that! I am a fellow servant with you and with your brothers and sisters who hold to the testimony of Jesus. Worship God! For it is the Spirit of prophecy who bears testimony to Jesus.'" (Revelation 19:10 NIV)*

DEMONS: FALLEN ANGELS IN REBELLION

Demons are angels who chose to rebel against God alongside Satan. Once part of God's heavenly host, they fell and became enemies of His purposes. Their nature and activity are revealed in Scripture:

1. They are called unclean or impure spirits:
"Just then a man in their synagogue who was possessed by an impure spirit cried out," (Mark 1:23 NIV)

2. They deceive, tempt, and accuse:
"The god of this age has blinded the minds of unbelievers, so that they cannot see the light of the gospel that displays the glory of Christ, who is the image of God." (2 Corinthians 4:4 NIV)

"The great dragon was hurled down—that ancient serpent called the devil, or Satan, who leads the whole world astray. He was hurled to the earth, and his angels with him. Then I heard a loud voice in heaven say: "Now have come the salvation and the power and the kingdom of our God, and the authority of his Messiah. For the accuser of our brothers and sisters, who accuses them before our God day and night, has been hurled down." (Revelation 12:9–10 NIV)

3. Their aim is to afflict, oppress, and torment, and in many cases, the ultimate objective is to completely possess.
Scripture provides a sobering illustration of this reality in the account of the demon-possessed man in the region of the Gerasenes:

"This man lived in the tombs, and no one could bind him anymore, not even with a chain. For he had often been chained hand and foot, but he tore the chains apart and broke the irons on his feet. No one was strong enough to subdue him. Night and day among the tombs and in the hills he would cry out and cut himself with stones......" (Mark 5:3–5 NIV)

Where angels serve God's will, demons serve Satan's schemes, aiming to destroy what God loves—especially humanity, who bear His image. Their power is real, but it is limited by God's authority and broken by the victory of Christ.

SPIRITS: FOUR DISTINCT CATEGORIES

The Bible uses the word *spirit* (*pneuma*) to describe different types of supernatural beings and realities. Not all spirits are the same, but understanding their categories helps us discern their influence.

1. *The Holy Spirit* – The third Person of the Trinity, who guides, teaches, convicts, and empowers believers (John 14:26; 16:13).
2. *The Human Spirit* – The eternal part of a person that continues after death, either in God's presence or separated from Him (Ecclesiastes 12:7; Matthew 13:42–43).
3. *Evil Spirits* – Demons or unclean spirits that oppose God, seeking to deceive and destroy (Mark 1:23–26).
4. *Angelic Spirits* – God's messengers and warriors, serving His purposes (Hebrews 1:14).

Not all spirits are angels, but all angels are spirits. Each operates according to its allegiance—either to God or against Him.

SPIRITUAL INFLUENCE ON HUMAN BEHAVIOR

The Influence of the Holy Spirit

- **Leads believers into all truth:**
  "But when He, the Spirit of truth, comes, He will guide you into all the truth. He will not speak on his own; He will

speak only what He hears, and He will tell you what is yet to come." (John 16:13 NIV)

- **Produces Godly fruit:**
  "love, joy, peace, patience, kindness, goodness, faithfulness, gentleness, and self-control" (Galatians 5:22–23).

- **Empowers believers to live as children of God**:
  "For those who are led by the Spirit of God are the children of God." (Romans 8:14).

- **Transforms hearts and renews minds:**
  "Do not conform to the pattern of this world, but be transformed by the renewing of your mind. Then you will be able to test and approve what God's will is—his good, pleasing and perfect will." (Romans 12:2 NIV)

The Influence of Evil Spirits

- **They seek to steal, kill, and destroy:**
  "The thief comes only to steal and kill and destroy; I have come that they may have life, and have it to the full." (John 10:10 NIV).

- **Deceive and blind minds to God's truth:**
  "The god of this age has blinded the minds of unbelievers, so that they cannot see the light of the gospel that displays the glory of Christ, who is the image of God." (2 Corinthians 4:4).

- **Provoke fear, torment, idolatry, addiction, and destruction:**
  "Be alert and of sober mind. Your enemy the devil prowls around like a roaring lion looking for someone to devour." (1 Peter 5:8 NIV) and "For our struggle is not against flesh

and blood, but against the rulers, against the authorities, against the powers of this dark world and against the spiritual forces of evil in the heavenly realms." (Ephesians 6:12 NIV).

In extreme cases, possess unsaved individuals, as in the account of the Gerasene demoniac (Mark 5:1–20). Spiritual influence is real and ongoing. Yet believers are not left powerless. Through the indwelling presence of the Holy Spirit, the truth of God's Word, and the authority given to us in Christ, we are fully equipped to discern, resist, and overcome demonic influence—walking daily in the victory He has already secured.

THE FLESH AND HUMAN FREE WILL

It is important to recognize that not all sin originates with demonic activity. While demonic forces tempt, torment, accuse, and exploit, much of what we wrestle with comes from within—the fallen human nature Scripture calls the flesh. Paul describes this pull vividly:

"For I know that good itself does not dwell in me, that is, in my sinful nature. For I have the desire to do what is good, but I cannot carry it out. For I do not do the good I want to do, but the evil I do not want to do—this I keep on doing."—Romans 7:18–20 (NIV)

The flesh is the inward pull toward selfishness, corruption, and independence from God. It does not require demonic influence to function, for since the fall in the Garden, it has been inherently predisposed toward sin. The flesh remains unredeemed and will not be transformed until Jesus returns. Until that day, we are called to grow in spiritual maturity so that we can deny its desires and walk in step with the Spirit.

"So I say, walk by the Spirit, and you will not gratify the de-

sires of the flesh. For the flesh desires what is contrary to the Spirit, and the Spirit what is contrary to the flesh. They are in conflict with each other, so that you are not to do whatever you want." — (Galatians 5:16–17 NIV)

This inner war reveals itself through lust, greed, pride, envy, and every other expression of selfishness. James reminds us that temptation does not begin outside of us but within:

"Each person is tempted when they are dragged away by their own evil desire and enticed." —(James 1:14 NIV)

In other words, not every failure is the result of a spiritual attack. Sometimes we fall simply because our flesh is weak, and we have not submitted it to the Spirit. If we do not mature spiritually, the flesh will continue to have its way.

MOVING ON

The key to walking faithfully in this unseen conflict is not fear but awareness, discernment, and dependence on Christ. We do not fight for victory—we fight from victory. As we surrender daily to the Spirit's leadership, resist the enemy's schemes, and guard against the pull of the flesh, we stand firm in the triumph of Jesus.

In the chapters ahead, we will explore how this invisible war plays out in practical ways—how spiritual gateways are opened, how strongholds are built, and most importantly, how the authority of Christ closes every door and restores freedom.

Prayer

Lord Jesus, thank You that the unseen battle is real, but the victory is already won. You have disarmed the powers of darkness and triumphed at the cross. I invite You to sharpen my discernment, guard my heart, and renew my mind. Help me to resist the enemy, stand firm in Your authority, and live clothed in the armor of God. Holy Spirit, fill me daily with Your presence and power, that I may walk not in fear but in victory. Amen.

Reflection Questions

What stood out to you about Satan's fall and the beginning of this invisible war?

1. In what ways have you noticed spiritual influence—whether angelic protection, demonic attack, or the pull of the flesh—in your own life?
2. How does knowing Christ's victory at the cross change the way you view spiritual warfare?
3. What practices can help you stay alert and discerning without falling into fear or obsession?
4. Where do you sense the Spirit inviting you to walk more fully in awareness and authority?

Chapter 5
WE LIVE IN THE SPIRITUAL REALM

*"And having disarmed the powers and authorities,
he made a public spectacle of them, triumphing
over them by the cross."— Colossians 2:15 (NIV)*

Human beings are not passive observers of the spiritual realm—we are active participants within it. Scripture reveals that we are spiritual vessels: eternal spirits housed in physical bodies, with souls that think, feel, and choose. Because of this design, we are never spiritually neutral. We are either filled and led by the Spirit of God or, by default, become vulnerable to the influence of the enemy. When we fail to intentionally connect with the Holy Spirit and live under His covering, we leave ourselves open to opposing forces. Recognizing this truth is vital, for the spiritual realm is neither distant nor abstract—it is ever-present, pressing at the door, seeking to shape our thoughts, desires, and actions in both subtle and profound ways.

THE ENEMY IS A THIEF & A LIAR

Jesus described the enemy as a thief. Just as burglars exploit unguarded doors, unlocked windows, or inattentive homeowners, the enemy looks for spiritual vulnerabilities in our lives. His aim is always the same—to steal what God has given, kill what carries life, and destroy what reflects God's image. He is opportunistic, waiting for moments of carelessness, trauma, compromise, or pain to create an opening and he will lie his way in. Awareness, truth, and Christ's covering serve as our locks and alarms. Without them, the enemy gains access.

Permission—whether through sin, wounds, generational patterns, or agreement with lies—grants him "legal ground" to intrude. Yet the thief's power is limited; he cannot force entry into a life sealed by Christ unless we grant it through agreement or neglect.

> *"The thief comes only to steal and kill and destroy; I have come that they may have life, and have it to the full." (John 10:10 NIV)*

> *"You belong to your father, the devil, and you want to carry out your father's desires. He was a murderer from the beginning, not holding to the truth, for there is no truth in him. When he lies, he speaks his native language, for he is a liar and the father of lies." (John 8:44 NIV)*

THE DANGER OF SPIRITUAL UNAWARENESS

To ignore the reality of the spiritual realm is like leaving your front door wide open in a dangerous neighborhood. Unawareness creates an invitation for deception, oppression, or bondage.

> *"Be alert and of sober mind. Your enemy the devil prowls around like a roaring lion looking for someone to devour." (1 Peter 5:8 NIV)*

> *"Above all else, guard your heart, for everything you do flows from it." (Proverbs 4:23 NIV)*

Awareness is the first safeguard, and discernment is the ongoing defense. Recognizing gateways allows us to close them quickly before the enemy takes advantage. Truth acts like a shield, exposing deception. Discernment functions like a spiritual alarm system, warning us when something is off. Together, they keep the doors of our lives secured under Christ's authority.

As we reflect on these areas, we can see that they closely align with the soul-level issues we have already explored. They overlap, and in many ways, they become the very openings through which the enemy attempts to gain access. This is why it is so important that we approach healing as a holistic journey—one that addresses the body, soul, and spirit together. When one area is left unattended, it can influence the others.

The enemy's influence in our lives is not random; it often finds its footing through places of unhealed pain, distorted beliefs, and unmet needs. Where there is wounding, there can be vulnerability. Where there are lies we have come to believe, there can be agreement. And where there has been prolonged disconnection—from God, from others, or even from our own hearts—there can be openings that need to be lovingly restored and brought back into alignment with truth.

THE IMPACT OF SIN AND VIOLATION

Violations against the soul often become places of vulnerability—spaces where pain, confusion, and distorted beliefs can take root. If these wounds are left unhealed, they can grow into patterns of brokenness that affect how we think, relate, and live.

Healing begins by recognizing these areas with compassion and inviting God's restoring presence into each one.

1. The Sins of Others Against Us

At some point in life, most of us have been affected by the choices or actions of others. These violations—whether through abuse, betrayal, harsh words, or mistreatment—can leave deep wounds in the soul.

Over time, the pain from these experiences can shape how

we see ourselves, others, and even God. If left unhealed, these wounds can influence behaviors, relationships, and internal patterns that continue the cycle of brokenness.

Healing begins with awareness, honesty, and the courageous pursuit of God's healing solution. What was done to you is not your fault—but healing is now your invitation.

2. Our Own Choices

Our own decisions also have the power to shape our internal world. When we move outside of God's design, it can create consequences that affect us emotionally, relationally, and spiritually.

These patterns can show up as guilt, shame, addiction, disconnection, or behaviors that feel difficult to break. But there is always hope.

Through confession, repentance, and surrender, we can bring every area into the light and experience forgiveness, cleansing, and restoration.

> *"If we confess our sins, He is faithful and just and will forgive us our sins and purify us from all unrighteousness."*— *1 John 1:9*

3. Generational Patterns and Inherited Brokenness

Scripture acknowledges that patterns can be passed down through families—cycles such as addiction, abuse, fear, poverty, or relational dysfunction.

These patterns are often learned, modeled, and reinforced over time until they begin to feel "normal." They can carry both spiritual and emotional weight. Yet Scripture also makes it clear: these patterns are not your destiny.

> *"Christ redeemed us from the curse of the law by becoming a curse for us…"*— *Galatians 3:13*

In Christ, every cycle can be interrupted. When we bring

these patterns into the light, renounce them, and embrace God's truth, a new legacy can begin.

4. Trauma and Neglect

Not all wounds come from something that was done to us. Some come from what we did not receive but deeply needed.

Neglect, emotional absence, rejection, abandonment, or exposure to traumatic experiences can leave gaps in the soul—places where safety, attachment, and identity were never fully formed.

Jesus meets us tenderly in these places.

"He heals the brokenhearted and binds up their wounds."
— Psalm 147:3

His healing is not rushed or forced. It is patient, kind, and deeply restorative.

5. Cultural and Environmental Influences

We live in environments that constantly shape our thinking, desires, and beliefs. Messages from culture—about identity, worth, sexuality, success, and power—can slowly influence the way we see ourselves and others.

Without discernment, these influences can quietly distort truth and create internal confusion or bondage.

Healing includes learning to filter what we take in, renew our minds with truth, and align our lives with God's design.

6. Agreement with Lies

Every wound carries the potential for a lie to attach to it. These lies can sound like:

- *"I am unlovable."*
- *"I will never change."*
- *"I am not enough."*
- *"God has abandoned me."*

When we unknowingly agree with these lies, they begin to shape our identity, our expectations, and our behavior. Over time, they can become strongholds.

But Jesus is Truth—and His truth brings freedom.

> *"Then you will know the truth, and the truth will set you free." (John 8:32)*

GENERATIONAL INFLUENCE AND FREEDOM IN CHRIST

One of the most painful experiences is feeling trapped in patterns that seem to repeat across generations. Scripture acknowledges this reality, but it also gives us profound hope.

> *"The son will not share the guilt of the father… the righteousness of the righteous will be credited to them."*
> *— Ezekiel 18:20*

Generational influences may shape us, but they do not define us. Through Christ: patterns can be broken lies can be replaced with truth identities can be restored and a new legacy can begin.

When we bring our history into the light, renounce unhealthy agreements, and align with God's truth, we step into freedom—not only for ourselves, but for generations to come.

This is the essence of true deliverance: not merely breaking free for a moment but learning to remain free by walking in the strength and authority Christ has already secured. Freedom is not the absence of battle—it is the assurance of victory in the battle. And in Him, that victory is ours.

Prayer:

Lord Jesus, thank You that while the battle is real and the enemy is active, the victory has already been won. By Your cross,

You disarmed the powers of darkness. Teach us to stand in that victory, to resist lies with truth, and to walk in the power of Your Spirit. Clothe us with Your armor, strengthen us in faith, and anchor us in Your promises. Amen.

Meditation:

Find stillness. Picture yourself clothed in the armor of God. Lay every lie, fear, and accusation at Jesus' feet. Hear His words: "Peace I leave with you; my peace I give you." (John 14:27 NIV) Rest in His presence until your heart is anchored in Him.

Reflection Questions

1. Where do you see evidence of the spiritual realm in your daily life?
2. How have you recognized the enemy's influence—fear, accusation, confusion?
3. What Scriptures remind you of angelic protection and God's presence?
4. Are there open doors (sin, wounds, unforgiveness) the Spirit is showing you to close?
5. What daily practices help you remain clothed in the armor of God?

REFLECTION AND APPLICATION (LIFE-STORY INVENTORY)

Take time to prayerfully reflect on your own story and upbringing. These prompts are not for blame or judgment, but for awareness—because awareness is the first step toward cleansing the soul and sealing points of entry. Go into what the Bible calls your "secret place," remove distractions, and ask the Holy Spirit to take you on a journey back into your past, showing you:

As you move through these questions, remember this is not about blaming your past or labeling your family. This is about gently becoming aware of the environments and experiences that shaped your heart and beliefs.

Move slowly. Notice what stands out to you. You do not have to process everything at once. Jesus meets you with compassion in every place of your story.

Abuse (Physical, Emotional, Mental, Sexual, or Spiritual)

Reflect on your early environment. Did you experience abuse that harmed you, or witness a parent or family member harming someone else? Were you ever exposed to sexual experiences, conversations, or expectations before you were developmentally ready, or in ways that felt confusing, unsafe, or violating? (These experiences always require high-level trauma-informed support.)

Consider whether you were manipulated or controlled emotionally. Was God ever used as a source of guilt, fear, or shame in your upbringing? Were you given the freedom to think for yourself, or were you told how you should think and what you should believe?

Take a moment to notice how any of these experiences may still influence your thoughts, emotions, or relationships today.

Monetary Pressures

Think about the financial environment of your home. Did financial stress affect daily life? Were money problems frequently discussed or argued about? Were there times when basic needs were not fully met, or when you felt you lacked what your peers had?

Notice what beliefs you may have formed about safety, provision, or your value in connection with money.

Work / Family-Life Imbalance

Reflect on the presence and availability of your caregivers. Were one or both parents often absent or working long hours, leaving you to care for yourself or manage responsibilities beyond your age?

Consider how this may have shaped your sense of safety, belonging, or personal value.

Breakdowns in Communication

Think about emotional connection in your home. Were your parents emotionally available for communication, feedback, or support? Did you feel safe expressing your thoughts, feelings, and needs?

Notice how these early patterns may still affect your ability to communicate, trust, or be vulnerable today.

Divorce and Separation

Consider whether your parents separated or divorced during your upbringing. Were there ongoing threats of divorce or instability in the relationship? Did you ever feel responsible for the conflict or feel caught in the middle?

Reflect on how these experiences may have shaped your sense of security, attachment, or view of relationships.

Substance Abuse

Reflect on whether either of your parents struggled with drugs or alcohol in ways that disrupted the stability of the home.

Notice what patterns this may have created for you—such as fear, unpredictability, hyper-responsibility, or emotional guarding.

Mental Health Challenges

Consider whether either parent struggled with mental health challenges. Did you experience them as emotionally stable and safe, or unpredictable and unsafe?

Reflect on how this may have influenced your sense of emotional safety, stability, and trust.

Cultural Shifts

Think about the broader environment you were raised in. Did changing social norms or worldly values influence your family roles, identity development, or structure in ways that felt confusing or misaligned?

Consider what messages you received about identity, worth, gender roles, or purpose.

Technological Distractions

Reflect on the presence of media and technology in your home. Was there excessive use of television, devices, or social media that limited emotional availability and meaningful interaction within your family?

Notice how this may have impacted your experience of connection, attention, and being seen.

Lack of Support Systems

Think about your extended support network. Did you have extended family, mentors, or community support to help navigate challenges? Or did you feel isolated, unsupported, or on your own?

Reflect on where you may still feel the impact of isolation or lack of support today.

Lack of Spiritual Support

Consider the spiritual environment of your home. Was your home grounded in faith? Were you encouraged to pursue a personal relationship with Jesus? Did your home life shape your view of God in a positive or negative way?

Reflect on how your early spiritual environment may still influence your current view of God and your relationship with Him.

Chapter 6
CLEANSING THE TEMPLE

"Don't you know that you yourselves are God's temple and that God's Spirit dwells in your midst?"
— 1 Corinthians 3:16 (NIV)

To minister wisely in the areas of deliverance and soul care, believers must understand how spiritual influence operates and how it can affect the human heart, mind, and behavior. Scripture reveals that the enemy rarely begins with obvious control or dramatic manifestations. Instead, his strategies often develop gradually—beginning with subtle temptation, increasing through oppression, and sometimes progressing into deeper patterns of bondage if left unaddressed. Recognizing this progression helps us approach ministry with clarity, humility, and discernment. It keeps us from dismissing genuine spiritual struggles while also preventing us from attributing every difficulty to demonic activity. With this balanced understanding, believers can respond with wisdom, relying on the authority of Christ and the guidance of the Holy Spirit to bring truth, healing, and freedom.

THE MINISTRY OF DELIVERANCE

The ministry of deliverance and soul care is God-ordained, multi-faceted, and essential for every believer. In the Great Commission, Jesus gave His followers a clear mandate: proclaim the gospel, heal the sick, and set the captives free. This is not an optional ministry reserved for a select few, but a calling given to every disciple, every Christian. And with it, He promised that His presence and power would always accompany the mission.

> *"He said to them, "Go into all the world and preach the gospel to all creation. Whoever believes and is baptized will be saved, but whoever does not believe will be condemned. And these signs will accompany those who believe: In my name they will drive out demons; they will speak in new tongues; they will pick up snakes with their hands; and when they drink deadly poison, it will not hurt them at all; they will place their hands on sick people, and they will get well."(Mark 16:15–18 NIV)*

Deliverance is the work of Christ, carried out through believers to set His people free. Yet before we can walk in authority as His vessels and minister freedom to others, we must first experience that freedom ourselves. The one who ministers must be a cleansed vessel—a temple prepared for the indwelling presence of the Holy Spirit to dwell in and flow through. We cannot effectively impart to others what we have not first received.

CLEANSING BEGINS WITH THE INNER TEMPLE

Jesus described the man as a "house." He said:

> *"In fact, no one can enter a strong man's house without first tying him up. Then he can plunder the strong man's house."(Mark 3:27 NIV)*

Through this, He taught that deliverance involves binding the intruder and removing him, so that the house—the temple—

can be fully cleansed and restored for God's purposes. Cleansing involves addressing demonic influence as well as bringing sin, shame, and hidden wounds into the light—exposing them through truth and honesty. Whether the sin is something we have committed or something committed against us, only Jesus can reveal and remove the stain. He alone promises full cleansing and complete restoration.

At the same time, Scripture warns of one sin that cannot be forgiven: blasphemy against the Holy Spirit. Every other sin—lust, anger, greed, bitterness—can be washed away, but blasphemy against the Holy Spirit remains unforgivable. This sin is the act of attributing the work of the Holy Spirit to Satan and persistently rejecting His witness about Christ. We see this clearly in the response of the Pharisees as Jesus was casting out demons:

> *"But when the Pharisees heard this, they said, 'It is only by Beelzebul, the prince of demons, that this fellow drives out demons.'" (Matthew 12:24 NIV)*

> *"And the teachers of the law who came down from Jerusalem said, 'He is possessed by Beelzebul! By the prince of demons he is driving out demons.'" (Mark 3:22 NIV)*

Jesus responded to their accusations:

> *"Truly I tell you, people can be forgiven all their sins and every slander they utter, but whoever blasphemes against the Holy Spirit will never be forgiven; they are guilty of an eternal sin." (Mark 3:28–29 NIV):*

The religious leaders claimed that Jesus' authority over demons came from *Beelzebul* (another name associated with Satan), instead of recognizing His power as coming from God. Jesus exposed the absurdity of their claim:

"Every kingdom divided against itself will be ruined... If Satan drives out Satan, he is divided against himself" (Matthew 12:25–26).

This reminds us that cleansing is not simply about outward behavior but about yielding inwardly to the Holy Spirit who sanctifies us.

THE WORD AS THE FOUNDATION: LOGOS AND RHEMA

Deliverance and soul care are not simply mechanical rituals or formulas. They are rooted in a relationship with Jesus through His Spirit and His Word. As we already learned in Chapter 1, God has given us both the written Word (*Logos*) and the spoken, personal Word of His Spirit (*Rhema*). In deliverance ministry, we need both.

- *Logos* ensures that we do not drift into error.
- *Rhema* ensures that our faith is alive and personal, not merely intellectual.

A minister who clings only to *Logos* risks becoming rigid and powerless, bound to the letter of the law. One who relies only on *Rhema* risks drifting into emotionalism or deception. Only together do they ground us in both truth and Spirit.

DISCERNMENT: THE KEY TO MINISTERING FREEDOM

Discernment is essential in deliverance; without it, we risk wounding the very ones we are trying to help. True discernment is more than suspicion or intuition—it is a Holy Spirit–given ability to see beneath the surface. Scripture commands us to test the spirits, and this is only truly possible through *Rhema*—the living voice and presence of the Holy Spirit dwelling within us.

Discernment helps us:

- Distinguish between fleshly sin (Romans 7:18–20; Galatians 5:16–17). Not every battle is demonic; sometimes the issue is simply the carnal nature at work.
- Identify wounds of the soul, which can act as open doors. Trauma, rejection, and neglect can create footholds the enemy exploits.
- Detect demonic influence when present. Spirits of fear, shame, heaviness, pride, or lust often hide behind wounds or habits, masquerading as personality traits.

Jesus demonstrated perfect discernment. He discerned that a woman bent over for eighteen years was afflicted not just with infirmity but with a "spirit of weakness."

> *"and a woman was there who had been crippled by a spirit for eighteen years. She was bent over and could not straighten up at all." (Luke 13:11 NIV)*

At other times, He simply forgave sin or healed without mentioning a spirit. Discernment allowed Him to minister precisely what was needed. This same gift is given to believers through the indwelling presence of Holy Spirit:

> *"to another miraculous powers, to another prophecy, to another distinguishing between spirits, to another speaking in different kinds of tongues, and to still another the interpretation of tongues."(1 Corinthians 12:10).*

EXORCISM VS. DELIVERANCE

Exorcism is the casting out of demons in Jesus' name. The Gospels are filled with examples:

- "Be quiet! Come out of him!" (Mark 1:25) — with a word, Jesus expelled the spirit.
- In Luke 8, He cast out a legion of demons from the man in the Gerasenes.

Exorcism demonstrates the power of the name of Jesus. But Jesus warned in Matthew 12:43–45 that if the "house" is swept clean but left empty, the spirit returns with others more wicked than itself. Exorcism without discipleship and inner healing risks leaving people worse off than before.

Deliverance, by contrast, is broader. It is freedom and wholeness—not just the removal of evil spirits but the restoration of the whole person. Deliverance involves:

- Filling the person with the Holy Spirit.
- Healing wounds that left openings.
- Breaking strongholds of lies and fear.
- Renouncing agreements with sin.
- Removing generational curses
- Closing doors, sealing the temple, removing spirit access.

It is important to remember that deliverance is not only about what is removed, but also about what is established in its place once what should not be there has been eliminated.

LEVELS OF AFFLICTION

Scripture and church history describe progressive stages of enemy influence. These stages help us understand how the enemy operates, how his tactics escalate, and why discernment is so crucial. Recognizing them keeps us from over-spiritualizing every struggle (blaming demons for everything) or underestimating real demonic activity (ignoring the unseen battle).

1. Temptation – External Suggestion

Temptation is the most common and universal form of spiritual influence. It often begins with subtle suggestions meant to draw us away from obedience to God. Discernment is essential, helping us distinguish between demonic influence and our own self-talk—the evil desires of the flesh.

Biblical Example: Satan tempted Jesus in the wilderness (Matthew 4:1–11). He used Scripture itself, twisting it to provoke compromise.

How It Operates: "First party" whispers of doubt appearing as self-talk ("Did God really say?"), enticements toward lust, greed, fear, or pride.

Fact: Temptation itself is not sin—it can lead to sin when we entertain it or come into agreement with it. James 1:14 explains, "Each person is tempted when they are dragged away by their own evil desire Victory is found by resisting with the Word of God, prayer, and through the surrender and submission to the Holy Spirit. With Jesus, we have discernment, built-in conviction and the power to resist.

2. Oppression – External Weight or Harassment

Oppression goes beyond suggestion; it is an external pressure weighing heavily on a person's mind, emotions, or circumstances.

Biblical Example: Acts 10:38 describes Jesus as the One who "went around doing good and healing all who were under the power of the devil."

How It Operates: Persistent heaviness, recurring setbacks, unusual resistance when pursuing godly goals, or cycles of despair and fatigue. Oppression is real, but it remains external—like a storm pressing against the walls of the soul. Victory is found in breaking oppression through intimacy with Jesus, worship, prayer, fasting, and standing in faith against the enemy's schemes (Ephesians 6:10–18).

3. Obsession / Strongholds – Entrenched Lies and Compulsions

If temptation and oppression are not resisted, they can evolve into obsession or strongholds—patterns of thought and behavior that dominate life.

Biblical Example: Paul describes strongholds as "arguments and every pretension that sets itself up against the knowledge of God" (2 Corinthians 10:4–5).

How It Operates:
- Lies believed as truth ("I will always fail," "God could never love me").
- Addictive or compulsive behaviors (pornography, rage, overspending, substance abuse, alcoholism).
- Emotional loops of fear, shame, or bitterness.

A stronghold eventually becomes a prison within. They are not formed merely through temptation, but through repeated reliance on false comforts (idols) and continual agreement with lies—patterns that reinforce bondage until truth breaks the cycle.

Victory is found by demolishing lies with truth, repentance, renewing the mind through Scripture, and inner healing to address root wounds. When Light is brought in, what is not supposed to be is exposed and pushed out. Only light can dispel darkness. In the natural world, darkness cannot exist where light is present. When a light is turned on in a dark room, the darkness instantly, in somewhat equal proportion, must leave—not because it fights back, but because it has no substance of its own. Darkness is simply the absence of light.

4. Demonization – Direct Spiritual Influence

Demonization refers to varying degrees of direct demonic activity affecting specific areas of a person's life. The Greek word *daimonizomai*, often translated as "possessed," is better understood as "to be demonized" or influenced.

Biblical Example: In Luke 13:11–16, a woman was crippled by a "spirit of infirmity" for eighteen years. Jesus discerned the spiritual root and set her free.

How It Operates:
- Torment in the mind (intrusive thoughts, confusion, suicidal ideation).
- Torment in emotions (uncontrollable anger, despair, tormenting fear).
- Torment in the body (infirmities or afflictions with no medical cause).

A Christian may experience demonic influence or oppression affecting the soul or body, but cannot be possessed in spirit, because the Holy Spirit dwells in the believer's innermost being. Where the Spirit of God resides, demonic ownership is impossible.

True victory is found through deliverance, awareness, repentance, renunciation, inner healing, and being filled with the Holy Spirit. There is only One who can fully expose deeply rooted lies, disclose hidden wounds, remove their power, and bring lasting healing to the soul—the Holy Spirit Himself.

5. Possession (Unbelievers Only) – Total Control of Will and Actions

Possession represents the deepest level of affliction, when a person yields complete control to demonic forces.

Biblical Example: The Gerasene man in Mark 5:1–20, who lived among tombs, exhibited supernatural strength, self-harm, and a loss of personal identity ("My name is Legion..... for we are many"). in Luke 8:30 (NIV) Jesus asked him, "What is your name?" "Legion," he replied, because many demons had gone into him. Both verses emphasize the concept of spiritual occupation — that the man was tormented not by a single unclean spirit, but by a multitude. Jesus' authority over "many" demonic forces demonstrates that no matter how great the oppression, His power to deliver is greater still.

How It Operates:
- Seizure of speech and actions.
- Overt supernatural manifestations (strength, voices, violence).
- Ongoing loss of rational control.

Possession is possible only in unbelievers. Believers are sealed by the Spirit (Ephesians 1:13) and "bought at a price" (1 Corinthians 6:20) and are no-longer their own.

Exorcism in Jesus' name, followed by salvation, deliverance, and discipleship to ensure the "house" is filled with the Holy Spirit and not left vulnerable.

Why Understanding Progression Matters

- Discernment is needed to understand at a deeper level what we are dealing with. Only our Lord knows for sure.
- Temptation can be resisted before it grows roots.
- Oppression can be lifted by resisting the enemy and turn-

ing to Christ.
- Obsession/Strongholds require truth to replace lies and inner healing for wounds.
- Demonization calls for deliverance ministry under the Holy Spirit's possession reveals the tragic extent of rebellion against God, but even here, Jesus has authority to bring freedom.

Understanding these stages helps us minister with wisdom—neither trivializing spiritual warfare nor sensationalizing it. The goal is always the same: healing, wholeness and freedom in Christ.

DEMONIZATION VS. POSSESSION

The Greek word *daimonizomai* means "to be demonized," not "possessed." *Demonization* refers to the varying levels of influence and harassment, while possession describes total takeover.

Demonization (Believers Can Experience):
- Partial influence in mind, emotions, or body.
- Christians can be oppressed, tormented, or hindered, but not owned.
-

Possession (Unbelievers Only):
- Complete control of the will, body, and speech.
- Possible only in those without the indwelling Holy Spirit.

Believers belong to Christ: "You are not your own; you were bought at a price" (1 Corinthians 6:19–20). They may need deliverance from influence, but they cannot be possessed.

THE ROLE OF COUNSELING AND INNER HEALING

Deliverance ministry is not a substitute for counseling and inner healing—it works best alongside them. True freedom is holistic. Jesus came not only to cast out demons but also to heal the brokenhearted and restore the soul (Luke 4:18). For this reason, deliverance, counseling, and inner healing must work together like interwoven strands of the same cord.

COUNSELING: RENEWING THE MIND AND WALKING OUT CHANGE

Counseling provides practical tools and guided support for growth. A counselor helps individuals:

- Uncover and process trauma and grief in safe, structured ways.
- Identify unhealthy thought patterns and behaviors that perpetuate cycles of pain.
- Develop new skills and strategies for communication, relationships, and emotional regulation.
- Rebuild a sense of safety and stability in areas damaged by abuse or neglect.

While counseling alone cannot cast out a demon, it equips a person to walk in greater wholeness after deliverance. It bridges the gap between spiritual freedom and the practical steps of living it out daily.

INNER HEALING: BRINGING JESUS INTO WOUNDED PLACES

Inner healing focuses on inviting Jesus into the broken, hidden, and often forgotten places of the soul. This ministry is about more than knowledge—it is about encounter. Inner healing helps individuals:

- Revisit painful memories with Jesus' presence, allowing Him to speak truth where lies once took root.
- Restore fractured places of the soul, bringing integration where there was fragmentation.
- Release forgiveness and receive comfort, breaking the chains of bitterness and resentment.
- Close the doors the enemy exploited, ensuring that wounds no longer serve as gateways for torment.

Where counseling may bring insight, inner healing invites transformation. The Holy Spirit brings revelation and freedom that no human wisdom alone can provide.

DELIVERANCE: REMOVING THE INTRUDER

Exorcism alone may remove a spirit, but without healing, the wound remains open. Counseling alone may bring insight, but without deliverance, the spiritual bondage remains intact.

Deliverance ensures that what has oppressed or demonized a person is removed by the power and authority of Jesus.

WORKING TOGETHER

When these three work in harmony, freedom is sustained and multiplied:
- Deliverance removes the intruder.
- Inner healing mends the wound and closes the door.
- Counseling equips the believer to walk in new patterns of truth and life.

This threefold approach reflects the ministry of Jesus Himself:

- He cast out demons (deliverance).
- He healed the brokenhearted (inner healing).
- He taught the crowds and discipled His followers (counseling and practical transformation).

By integrating these, believers can experience not only breakthrough but lasting freedom.

"MY HOUSE:" WHY SPIRITS SEEK TO RE-ENTER

Jesus provides a sobering picture of spiritual realities in Luke 11:24–26 and Matthew 12:43–45. An unclean spirit goes out from a person and later says, "I will return to my house." Finding the house swept, put in order, yet empty, it returns with seven spirits more wicked than itself, leaving the person worse off. Important factors:

- Unclean spirits seek habitation, with their goal being full possession, not just influence.
- Expelled spirits are smart, they know where they came from, they know their way back, and they attempt reentry.
- An empty house is vulnerable.
- True deliverance must be followed by discipleship and Spirit-filled living.

Freedom is not merely removal; it is replacement. Bring in light, in somewhat equal proportion, dispels the darkness. Yield every room of the heart to the rule of Jesus.

> *"When an impure spirit comes out of a person, it goes through arid places seeking rest and does not find it. Then it says, 'I will return to the house I left.' When it arrives, it finds the house unoccupied, swept clean and put in order."* (Matthew 12:43–45 NIV)

CHAPTER 5

Reflection Questions
1. Where do you see temptation, oppression, or strongholds in your own life?
2. Do you recognize the difference between fleshly struggles and demonic influence?
3. Are there wounds or lies from your past that still need inner healing?
4. Have you made room for the Holy Spirit to fill the "house" of your soul?
5. How can you grow in discernment to minister freedom to others?

Prayer
Lord Jesus, thank You that You came to set captives free. Search my heart and reveal any footholds or strongholds of the enemy. Heal my wounds, break strongholds, and close every open door. Fill me with Your Spirit so that every part of my life is surrendered to You. Teach me to discern wisely and to minister freedom with compassion and truth. I declare that my life fully belongs to You, and I choose to walk in Your victory. In Jesus name' - Amen

Chapter 7
GOD AS JUDGE & REDEEMER

"Let us then approach God's throne of grace with confidence, so that we may receive mercy and find grace to help us in our time of need." (Hebrews 4:16 NIV)

All of God's creation was made for relationship with the Creator, Redeemer, and Giver of Life—moving from being His precious creation to becoming His precious child. Knowing Jesus personally does not diminish the reality that God is both holy and just. Scripture reveals Him as the Supreme Judge and the Merciful Redeemer—perfectly righteous in judgment and unfailing in mercy. He is the sovereign authority who raises up one and brings another down:

> *"It is God who judges: He brings one down, He exalts another."*
> *(Psalm 75:7, NIV)*

> *"...You have come to God, the Judge of all, to the spirits of the righteous made perfect." (Hebrews 12:23, NIV)*

As Judge, His verdicts are final and unquestionable. Yet the paradox of the gospel is that the Judge also sits on the Mercy Seat. Judgment and mercy are not contradictory in Him; they meet at the cross. At Calvary, Jesus absorbed the judgment our sins deserved so that God could extend mercy without compromising justice. Because of this, when believers approach His throne, they no longer find wrath but grace in their time of need. This is the solution to humanity's greatest problem: a holy God whose justice demands judgment, yet whose love provides mercy through His Son.

> *"Let us then approach God's throne of grace with confidence, so that we may receive mercy and find grace to help us in our time of need." (Hebrews 4:16 NIV)*

LEGAL RIGHTS AND THE COURTROOM OF HEAVEN

Understanding God as Judge and Redeemer helps us grasp the depth of the freedom He offers. One of the most effective tools the enemy uses against us is the system of legal rights and agreements we unknowingly make with him. Many believers live under these lies daily without realizing it. If our lives were examined in a spiritual courtroom, the enemy would present these agreements as binding evidence against us—evidence that seems to prove guilt. These agreements function like inner scripts playing in the background, shaping identity and behavior.

While God is the supreme Judge, the accuser still has a voice in the courtroom of heaven. He twists God's Word, stripping it of grace, and uses it to condemn. He claims jurisdiction over sins, failures, and wrongdoings, but his accusations go even deeper—attacking identity and worth. These lies keep people bound in cycles of shame and self-condemnation, even when forgiveness has already been secured by Christ.

Yet the gospel reminds us that we have an Advocate with the Father—Jesus Christ, the Righteous One (1 John 2:1). In Him, every accusation loses its power, every legal claim is dismissed, and every false verdict is overturned. To walk in this reality, we must face the truth of the agreements we have made and bring them under the authority of Christ.

THE COURTROOM OF HEAVEN

The concept of a courtroom might seem like a purely human invention—something born out of modern systems like the American justice model. In truth, however, the very idea of legal standing originates from God Himself. Earthly courts are merely a reflection of the heavenly order, where righteousness, justice, and truth form the foundation of His throne. Let's look at some key areas of scripture that highlight this truth:

- *"The court was seated, and the books were opened." Heaven has records, verdicts, and decrees. God's judgments are rendered in His courts. —Daniel 7:10*
  Daniel is being shown that human and demonic powers don't get the last word. Even when evil kingdoms seem unstoppable (the "beasts" in Daniel 7), God's court will sit, truth will be revealed, and His justice will be executed.

- *"The accuser of our brothers and sisters, who accuses them before our God day and night, has been hurled down. They triumphed over him by the blood of the Lamb and by the word of their testimony." The blood of Jesus cancels the enemy's claims, and our testimony affirms agreement with God's verdict. Revelation 12:10–11*
  Satan's primary weapon here is accusation: condemnation, shame, guilt, and spiritual intimidation. This verse is a victory announcement in the middle of a spiritual war. It explains what changes when Satan is cast down and how believers overcome his attacks.

- *"Let us then approach God's throne of grace with confidence, so that we may receive mercy and find grace to help us in our time of need." This is courtroom language—entering boldly, assured that our case has already been won through Christ. Hebrews 4:16*
Because Jesus understands our weaknesses and represents us before the Father, we don't have to run from God when we struggle—we can run to Him. The throne we fear becomes the throne where we're helped. When we're tempted, overwhelmed, ashamed, anxious, or under attack, Hebrews 4:16 is permission to pray immediately—not after we "get it together." God's mercy covers us, and His grace empowers us.

- *"For the Lord is our judge, the Lord is our lawgiver, the Lord is our king; it is He who will save us." Jesus holds the key to freedom. Isaiah is saying: God is in control, God sets the truth, God reigns, and God rescues. We don't need to look to any other authority for security. God is the One who rules rightly, leads faithfully, and saves completely. Isaiah 33:22*

The heavenly legal system existed long before earthly courtrooms were ever established. In fact, earthly justice is merely a faint reflection of the eternal justice of God.

Yet there is one bold, beautiful difference between the courtroom of the world and the courtroom of Heaven: grace. Grace is the judicial system of Heaven. It is God's provision to take upon Himself the punishment we deserved. There is no greater weapon of warfare than grace.

When we receive Jesus and accept the power of grace, we admit our wrong to Him, and He steps into the courtroom on our behalf. He does not ignore sin or sweep it aside. God forbid. Instead, He upholds the highest standard against sin's devastation and destruction. This is why Jesus had to pay the price Himself. No other substitute would suffice. Either we would pay the penalty for our own wrongdoing, or the perfect sacrifice of Jesus would pay it for us.

When we believe in Jesus and accept His grace, the enemy's accusations lose all legal ground. Shame is broken, guilt is lifted, and condemnation is silenced. Not only are we released from punishment, but we are also connected to the full power and resources of God's majesty, goodness, and love.

WHAT ARE LEGAL RIGHTS?

Legal rights are the agreements we have made or someone else made for us—knowingly or unknowingly—in the spiritual realm that give the enemy permission to operate in our lives. They are the footholds that make his accusations, strategies, and influence appear valid. The enemy cannot bypass grace directly, but he works by convincing people that his claims are true and that the power of grace is either insufficient or inapplicable to them.

We must understand something crucial: we don't need to have committed the sin itself for a legal right to exist. Sometimes all it takes is our agreement with the lie that we deserve punishment, or that something other than the blood of Jesus can make us right with God. These agreements function as "contracts" in the spiritual realm. In other words, legal rights are any places where the flow of Jesus' grace has been blocked. They often stem from:

- *Unrepented Sin* – When we choose to cling to sin rather than surrender it to God, we give the enemy legal ground—territory he claims as his own.
- *Unforgiveness* – Holding onto offense or resentment opens a spiritual door for torment, as Jesus illustrated in (Matthew 18:34).

- *Lies and False Beliefs* – When we accept lies about God, ourselves, or others, we align with the accuser's narrative instead of God's truth.
- *Generational Agreements* – The sins and patterns passed down through our family line can form spiritual inheritances of bondage until they are broken by the finished work of the cross (Exodus 20:5–6).
- *Inner Vows and Self-Judgments* – Words spoken in pain, such as "I'll never trust anyone again," or "I'm unworthy of love," act as binding agreements that the enemy exploits to reinforce deception and division.

When we accept or tolerate a behavior, we are unknowingly coming into agreement with the spirit influencing it—opening the door for that same behavior to take root in our own lives. The enemy has no real authority except what we yield to him, which is why his greatest weapon is deception. If he can persuade us that we are guilty, hopeless, or beyond the reach of God's grace, we begin to live as though condemnation is our destiny—even though the cross has already secured our complete freedom.

Paul reminds us:

> *"In order that Satan might not outwit us. For we are not unaware of his schemes." (2 Corinthians 2:11 NIV)*

> *"Therefore, there is now no condemnation for those who are in Christ Jesus." — (Romans 8:1 NIV)*

Recognizing and breaking these legal rights is essential to walking in lasting freedom. When we confess and repent of the lies we've believed, and boldly declare the finished work of Christ, we dismantle every false claim of the enemy. In doing so, the flow of God's grace is restored to those areas of our lives, and the power of truth replaces the grip of deception.

1. God: The Righteous Judge

In the courtroom of Heaven, God alone oversees and mandates righteousness and truth. Scripture makes it clear that judgment belongs to Him:

> *"There is only one Lawgiver and Judge, the one who is able to save and destroy. But you—who are you to judge your neighbor?" (James 4:12)*

Human beings will never be granted the authority to judge themselves or one another, because the perfect standard required for judgment belongs to God alone. Only He possesses the holiness, wisdom, and purity necessary to render verdicts without error or partiality.

At the throne, holiness and grace converge. God never compromises His holiness by ignoring sin, nor does He compromise His love by condemning without offering hope. He rules as the Righteous Judge, where justice and mercy meet.

- His holiness ensures that sin is seen for what it truly is—rebellion, brokenness, and devastation.
- His grace extends redemption through Jesus Christ, the perfect substitute who bore our punishment, giving us what we do not deserve.
- His mercy withholds the judgment we do deserve—eternal separation from God—offering instead the gift of eternal life through Christ.

Oversight and Kingdom authority are the foundation of God's divine order. He alone is qualified to weigh every motive, expose every hidden place, and render the final verdict. For all who are in Christ, that verdict is already settled—forgiven, redeemed, and made righteous through the blood of the Lamb.

2. Jesus Christ: The Advocate and Defender

Jesus stands at our side as our Advocate. He does not deny the charges of sin, because sin is real and destructive. Instead, He points to His own blood as the evidence that the penalty has already been paid.

- Where the enemy cries, "Guilty!", Jesus declares, "Justified!"
- Where the accuser demands punishment, Jesus responds, "The debt is canceled!"
- Where shame says, "Unworthy!", Jesus proclaims, "Redeemed and beloved!"
  "If anybody does sin, we have an advocate with the Father—Jesus Christ, the Righteous One. He is the atoning sacrifice for our sins, and not only for ours but also for the sins of the whole world." (1 John 2:1–2)

The cross is His closing argument, and the verdict is unshakable: the believer is set free.

3. The Holy Spirit: The Witness

In every courtroom, testimony matters. The Holy Spirit takes the witness stand in the believer's heart. He confirms the truth of God's Word, convicts us of sin—not to condemn us but to bring us to repentance—and reassures us of our identity in Christ.

"The Spirit himself testifies with our spirit that we are God's children." (Romans 8:16)

His testimony silences the lies of the enemy by reminding us who we are in Him: forgiven, adopted, sealed, and empowered.

4. The Believer: The Defendant

We enter the heavenly courtroom carrying our petitions, confessions, and prayers—presenting ourselves humbly before God. We do not argue our own righteousness but stand in agreement with the righteousness of Christ. Our role is surrender. In this place of divine justice, we seek eviction notices and restraining orders against all ungodly spiritual activity, removing any legal right or access the enemy has gained, and reclaiming what rightfully belongs under the Lordship of Jesus Christ.

When we confess sin, repent of lies, and renounce false agreements, we are effectively saying, "I step out of agreement with the accuser and into agreement with the Advocate." Through repentance and faith, we align ourselves with heaven's order and receive God's verdict of freedom.

5. Satan: The Prosecutor

Satan, the accuser of the brethren, relentlessly brings charges against us day and night. He digs through our past, exploits our wounds, and exposes generational iniquities—all in an effort to establish legal grounds to afflict and oppress. His ultimate goal is to persuade both us and the heavenly court that grace no longer applies, attempting to undermine the finished work of Christ with accusation and deception.

> *"For the accuser of our brothers and sisters, who accuses them before our God day and night, has been hurled down." (Revelation 12:10)*

But his arguments collapse in the presence of Christ's blood. Every claim is silenced by the greater evidence of the cross.

WHY DOES THE COURTS OF HEAVEN MATTER

This perspective brings balance to deliverance. Sometimes, people think of it only as a battle of power: shout louder, pray harder, fast longer. But the truth is, when legal rights are removed, the enemy has no more claim. Deliverance is not about overpowering demons; it is about removing their grounds and enforcing Christ's victory.

The courtroom of heaven assures us of three key factors:
- The accuser does not have the final word.
- Our Advocate has already paid the price.
- The Judge delights to rule in our favor because of Christ.

When we truly grasp this truth, we stop striving for freedom and begin standing in the freedom already secured for us through Christ. Deliverance then becomes less about a dramatic encounter and more about a confident exchange of truth—a divine transaction sealed and sustained by the Holy Spirit.

IN CONCLUSION

Understanding the courtroom of heaven is not meant to create fear or legalistic striving. Instead, it reveals the beauty of the gospel and the depth of the freedom Christ has secured for us. God is not only the righteous Judge—He is also the Redeemer who provided the payment for our freedom through the sacrifice of His Son.

The enemy's accusations lose their power when we agree with God's truth. The moment we confess our sin, renounce lies, and place our trust in Jesus, the verdict has already been rendered.

The blood of Christ silences every accusation, cancels every debt, and restores our standing before God.

The goal of this understanding is not merely information—it is transformation. When believers grasp the reality of grace, they stop living under shame and condemnation and begin walking confidently in the freedom Christ has already secured.

Freedom begins when we step out of agreement with the accuser and fully into agreement with the Advocate.

As you reflect on what you have learned, take a moment to bring your heart before the Lord.

Reflection Questions

1. Are there areas in my life where I still feel condemned, ashamed, or unworthy—even though Christ has already secured my forgiveness?
2. Have I unknowingly come into agreement with lies about my identity, my worth, or God's grace?
3. Is there any sin, unforgiveness, inner vow, or false belief that may still be giving the enemy influence in my life?
4. Am I fully trusting in the finished work of Jesus, or do I still feel the need to earn God's acceptance?
5. What areas of my life need to be brought back under the authority and Lordship of Jesus Christ?
6. How can I more fully live in agreement with God's verdict over my life—that I am forgiven, redeemed, and made righteous through Christ?

Take a moment to speak honestly with God about anything He brings to your attention. His desire is not to condemn you, but to restore you and lead you into greater freedom.

Closing Prayer

Heavenly Father,

I come before You with humility and gratitude, knowing that through Jesus Christ the penalty for my sin has already been paid. Thank You that the accusations of the enemy have no authority over those who belong to You.

Lord, I confess any place where I have believed lies, held onto unforgiveness, or come into agreement with anything that is not aligned with Your truth. I renounce those agreements now and place them under the authority of Jesus Christ.

Thank You that the blood of Jesus speaks a better word over my life—one of forgiveness, redemption, and freedom. I receive Your mercy and grace, and I choose to walk in the truth of who You say I am.

Holy Spirit, lead me to live in the freedom Christ has secured for me and help me walk daily in Your truth. In Jesus' name, Amen.

Chapter 8
DISCERNING SPIRITUAL CONDITIONS

*"Submit yourselves, then, to God. Resist the devil,
and he will flee from you."— James 4:7 (NIV)*

Every day, we face the reality of spiritual conflict and must decide which kingdom we will align ourselves with—in thought, word, and action. This initial choice is deeply personal; no one else can make it for us. In His kindness, Jesus has given each of us the gift of free will—the ability to choose whom we will serve. He has placed us at the helm of our own vessel, granting both the privilege and the responsibility to steer our lives in the direction of our choosing. Yet refusing to choose is, in itself, a choice—one that defaults to the enemy's domain. Still, we must understand this truth: even after receiving His gift of eternal life, we can experience a kind of hell on earth if we fail to surrender to Him daily—walking with Him, growing in Him, and allowing His presence to transform us and guide our every step. Just as darkness is merely the absence of light, so evil is the absence of God.

Jesus made this truth unmistakably clear when He said:

"Whoever is not with me is against me, and whoever does not gather with me scatters." (Matthew 12:30 NIV)

"If you belonged to the world, it would love you as its own. As it is, you do not belong to the world, but I have chosen you out of the world. That is why the world hates you." (John 15:19 NIV)

These verses remind us that neutrality is not an option in the spiritual realm. Our awareness is sharpened by recognizing that our daily choices—what we believe, speak, dwell on, and act upon—either reinforce the kingdom of God or give ground to the enemy.

Awareness, therefore, is not simply a mental note of good versus evil. It is a spiritual posture of vigilance. It means we are awake, alert, and discerning. The apostle Peter warned us with urgency:

"Be alert and of sober mind. Your enemy the devil prowls around like a roaring lion looking for someone to devour." (1 Peter 5:8 NIV)

Awareness does not mean living in fear, but it does mean refusing complacency. Spiritual blindness leaves us vulnerable, but awareness positions us to take hold of the authority Jesus has given us. We are equipped with discernment through the Holy Spirit, who exposes the enemy's schemes and strengthens us to resist.

SPIRITUAL BLINDNESS AND DECEPTION

The enemy preys upon spiritual blindness and ignorance. When we lack discernment or fail to recognize the reality of the battle, we become vulnerable to his schemes. Demonic forces wound the soul and then exploit those very wounds, fueling shame, doubt, and confusion. They twist truth into deception, crafting false narratives that distort our identity and lead us away from God's purpose.

SOLDIERS IN WARFARE

Just as earthly soldiers operate under ranks—generals, captains, lieutenants—spiritual warfare also involves a hierarchy. Paul reminds us in Ephesians 6:12 that our struggle is not against flesh and blood, but *"against rulers, against authorities, against the principalities and powers of this dark world and against the spiritual forces of evil in the heavenly realms."* These forces are organized, strategic, and relentless.

Within this unseen battle, certain spirits seem to operate with higher-ranking influence, directing or reinforcing lesser spirits. To recognize their nature is not to glorify them but to be equipped to stand against them in the authority of Christ, clothed in the armor of God. At the cross, Jesus disarmed principalities and powers (Colossians 2:15), yet believers are called to remain alert to the enemy's schemes so that we may resist him effectively.

Some of the most commonly recognized high-ranking spirits, identified both directly and indirectly in Scripture—and confirmed through experience in spiritual warfare—include the following:

The Strongman

The ruling spirit that guards a "house", maintaining control until bound.

"Or again, how can anyone enter a strong man's house and carry off his possessions unless he first ties up the strong man? Then he can plunder his house." (Matthew 12:29 NIV)

Imposter Spirits

These are deceptive spirits that mimic the voice, presence, or gifts of God in order to mislead. They often disguise themselves as holy or good, skillfully imitating the things of God to divert believers from truth and from a genuine, intimate relationship with Him. Their purpose is subtle deception—creating confusion, fostering counterfeit experiences, and drawing attention away from the true work of the Holy Spirit.

"And no wonder, for Satan himself masquerades as an angel of light. It is not surprising, then, if his servants also masquerade as servants of righteousness. Their end will be what their actions deserve." (2 Corinthians 11:14–15 NIV).

Dear friends, do not believe every spirit, but test the spirits to see whether they are from God, because many false prophets have gone out into the world." (1 John 4:1 NIV).

Familiar Spirits

These are demonic entities that attach themselves generationally or through occult involvement, exploiting knowledge of family history and behavioral patterns. The term "familiar spirit" appears multiple times in Scripture, particularly in the Old Testament, describing spirits that people would consult through mediums, necromancers, or divination practices. They are called "familiar" because they imitate the voices, personalities, or knowledge of the dead—deceiving individuals into believing they are communicating with lost loved ones or receiving hidden wisdom. A familiar spirit is a counterfeit guide, posing as a source of comfort or insight while secretly binding those who listen. It operates through false intimacy, using familiarity to manipulate and control. Over time, a person can become so accustomed to its influence that they mistake its input for their own thoughts—what may seem like harmless "self-talk" can, in truth, be spiritual deception. Scripture warns us to "take every thought captive to make it obedient to Christ", filtering all thoughts through the truth of God's Word before accepting or entertaining them.

"We demolish arguments and every pretension that sets itself up against the knowledge of God, and we take captive every thought to make it obedient to Christ." (2 Corinthians 10:5 NIV)

"Do not turn to mediums or seek out spiritists, for you will be defiled by them. I am the Lord your God." Leviticus 19:31 (NIV)

The Jezebel Spirit

A spirit of manipulation, control, and counterfeit authority, often operating in rebellion against God's order.

"Jezebel his wife said, 'Is this how you act as king over Israel? Get up and eat! Cheer up. I'll get you the vineyard of Naboth the Jezreelite.' So she wrote letters in Ahab's name... 'Seat two scoundrels opposite him and have them bring charges that he has cursed both God and the king. Then take him out and stone him to death.'" (1 Kings 21:7–10 NIV)

The Python Spirit

A constricting spirit associated with divination, oppression, and suffocating the flow of the Holy Spirit.

"Once when we were going to the place of prayer, we were met by a female slave who had a spirit by which she predicted the future. She earned a great deal of money for her owners by fortune-telling." (Acts 16:16 NIV).

The Leviathan Spirit

A twisting, prideful spirit that distorts communication, fosters division, and resists humility.

"Can you pull in Leviathan with a fishhook or tie down its tongue with a rope?... No one is fierce enough to rouse it—who then is able to stand against me?" (Job 41:1, 10 NIV).

Knowing their names is far less important than discerning their presence and being willing to confront them fearlessly as needed—through the authority granted to us by Jesus and the power of the Holy Spirit—as we carry out the Great Commission. These categories are not meant to inspire fear but to provide understanding of the types of opposition believers may face. The goal is discernment, not obsession—recognizing the fingerprints of the enemy so we can respond with wisdom, truth, and the spiritual authority we possess in Christ.

THE STRONGMAN

The strongman is a ruling spirit, the "gatekeeper" that controls a house—whether that house is a person's life, a family line, a community, or even a region. Jesus gave us this principle:

"Or again, how can anyone enter a strong man's house and carry off his possessions unless he first ties up the strong man? Then he can plunder his house." (Matthew 12:29)

In this passage, Jesus reveals that demonic forces do not act randomly or without structure. There is often a dominant spirit—a strongman—that exercises authority and control over a person or situation. This spirit gains and maintains its power through legal rights such as unrepented sin, unforgiveness, trauma, generational iniquity, or ungodly agreements. Surrounding it is a "family" of lesser minion spirits that work in unity to enforce its agenda and sustain the bondage.

How Strongmen Operate

- *Gatekeeping Authority* – The strongman acts as the ruling power over a person's "house" (life). Lesser spirits function under its command.
- *Legal Rights* – Access is often gained through unrepented sin, generational curses, unforgiveness, or occult involvement.
- *Enforcement of Bondage* – The strongman ensures cycles of sin, oppression, or torment remain unbroken.
- *Familial Network* – Rarely does a strongman work alone; it establishes a cluster of related spirits that strengthen its control.
- *Example:* A strongman of fear may bring with it anxiety, nightmares, torment, and distrust. A strongman of whoredoms may bring lust, pornography, and adultery.

The Strongman's Team

This list identifies several common strongmen and the families of spirits they oversee:
- *Spirit of Fear* (2 Timothy 1:7) can include anxiety, panic, nightmares, distrust, torment.
- *Spirit of Pride / Leviathan* (Job 41; Isaiah 27:1) can include arrogance, rebellion, strife, self-righteousness.
- *Spirit of Heaviness* (Isaiah 61:3) can include depression, despair, suicide, fatigue, hopelessness.
- *Spirit of Bondage* (Romans 8:15) can include addictions, compulsions, oppression, slavery to sin.
- *Spirit of Whoredoms* (Hosea 4:12) can include lust, immorality, pornography, adultery, perversion.
- *Spirit of Jezebel* (1 Kings 18–21; Revelation 2:20) can include manipulation, witchcraft, rebellion, false prophecy.
- *Spirit of Antichrist* (1 John 4:3) can include denial of Christ, deception, counterfeit religion.

Why Binding the Strongman Is Crucial

If we focus only on the lesser spirits—such as fear, anger, or lust—deliverance may be temporary. Unless the strongman is identified, confronted, and bound, it will eventually reestablish control and summon the others back in. This is why Jesus emphasized that the strongman must first be dealt with before true and lasting freedom can be secured.

THE IMPOSTER SPIRIT

An imposter spirit is a demonic influence that imitates the voice, behavior, or personality of an individual. It presents itself in familiar ways—sometimes even sounding like one's own inner voice—but its true intent is deception. Its purpose is to distort truth, confuse identity, and pull a person out of alignment with the Holy Spirit and the truth of God's Word. This spirit often counterfeits the voice of God, mimics spiritual gifts, or reproduces patterns of past trauma within a person's life. Its ultimate goal is division—separating a person from God, from others, and even from their own sense of identity and peace within the soul.

Entry Points of the Imposter Spirit

An imposter spirit gains access through "open doors" in a person's life—often during moments of vulnerability, trauma, or compromise. The five senses serve as potential gateways through which influence can enter, which is why believers must remain spiritually alert and guard these entry points against the enemy's access. Common contributors include:

- *Trauma* – Experiences of abuse, betrayal, neglect, or violence can fragment a person's identity. The imposter spirit often steps into these broken places, pretending to "speak" as the victim or protector, but instead reinforces lies of shame, fear, or anger.

- *Occult Involvement* – Practices such as séances, tarot, channeling, or witchcraft invite counterfeit spiritual voices. These open legal doors to spirits that impersonate loved ones, "spirit guides," or even the Holy Spirit.
- *Addiction / Idolatry* – Substance use, alcohol, pornography, or other compulsive behaviors can create spiritual openings, allowing the imposter spirit to enter and reinforce destructive patterns by whispering excuses, false comfort, or distorted cravings. These behaviors fall under the category of idolatry—anything we turn to for comfort, relief, or fulfillment that can and should only come from God becomes a false god in our lives.
- *Generational Sin and Curses* – Family patterns of deception, occult involvement, or false religion can invite familiar or imposter spirits that entrench themselves within a family's identity, perpetuating cycles of bondage across generations.

Scriptural Support

Though the Bible doesn't use the exact phrase "Imposter Spirit," several passages reveal the reality of spiritual mimicry and deception:

- *Mark 5:1–13* —The man possessed by Legion exhibited behavior entirely foreign to his true identity. Once delivered by Jesus, Scripture says he was "sitting there, dressed and in his right mind" (Mark 5:15, NIV), revealing that a legion of false personalities and demonic influences had been operating within him.
- *1 Timothy 4:1* — *"In later times some will abandon the faith and follow deceiving spirits and things taught by de-*

mons." These deceiving spirits mimic truth to draw people away from God.

- *2 Corinthians 11:14* — *"Satan himself masquerades as an angel of light." Demonic spirits can present themselves as good, wise, or spiritual, while leading into deception.*
- *Acts 16:16* — A slave girl carried a spirit of divination that mimicked prophecy. Paul discerned the counterfeit and cast it out. "Once when we were going to the place of prayer, we were met by a female slave who had a spirit by which she predicted the future."

Strategies of the Imposter Spirit

This spirit's main weapon is impersonation. It seeks to confuse and destabilize through:

- *Mimicking Voice or Personality*: It can sound like one's own thoughts or even impersonate the voice of a loved one in visions, dreams, or inner impressions.
- *False Guidance:* Pretends to offer "spiritual insight" but always steers away from God's Word, bringing confusion or compromise.
- *Accusation:* Poses as the person's own conscience but laces it with condemnation and shame. Instead of conviction that leads to repentance, it enforces guilt that leads to despair.
- *Division:* Drives wedges in relationships, whispering lies like "They don't love you," "You can't trust them," or "You're better off alone."
- *False Identity Overlays:* In cases of deep trauma, the imposter spirit may act like an "alternate personality," speaking or acting in ways contrary to the person's redeemed identity.

Effects of the Imposter Spirit

When active, this spirit often produces the following effects:
- *Confusion in identity* – creating an inner conflict where a person feels "two-faced" or as if they are battling different versions of themselves.
- *Shame and accusation* – fueling constant self-condemnation, guilt, and doubt.
- *Distorted self-perception* – convincing individuals to believe lies about who they are and how God sees them.
- *Relational conflict* – twisting perceptions and motives, causing mistrust and division in relationships.
- *Double-mindedness* – generating instability in decision-making, emotions, and faith.
- *Spiritual deception* – imitating the prophetic through counterfeit impressions, dreams, or voices that lead away from truth.

How to Discern the Imposter Spirit

The Bible instructs us to "test the spirits" (1 John 4:1). Discernment questions include:
- Does this voice or impression exalt Jesus Christ as Lord, or does it shift focus away from Him?
- Does it align with the fruit of the Spirit (Galatians 5:22–23) or produce fear, shame, and control?
- Does it speak truth according to Scripture, or twist God's Word for selfish gain?
- Does it convict in love, or condemn in despair?

THE FAMILIAR SPIRIT

A Familiar Spirit is a demonic entity that attaches itself to individuals, families, or even entire bloodlines with the intent to influence, deceive, and control through counterfeit familiarity.

The term "familiar" refers to intimate knowledge—these spirits carefully observe patterns, study behaviors, and exploit weaknesses over time. They become "familiar" with a person's history, wounds, and generational legacy, enabling them to operate subtly and often undetected unless discerned by the Holy Spirit. Even self-talk, if not properly tested and aligned with Scripture, can be influenced by a familiar spirit seeking to imitate one's own thoughts or inner voice.

In Scripture, the Hebrew word *'ôb* refers to mediums or spirits of the dead. These were connected to practices of necromancy and divination—attempts to communicate with the dead or seek hidden knowledge apart from God. Such practices were strictly forbidden by God because they open the door to demonic influence and deception.

Scriptural Warnings

- *Leviticus 19:31 (KJV) – "Regard not them that have familiar spirits, neither seek after wizards, to be defiled by them: I am the Lord your God."*
- *Leviticus 20:6 (KJV) – "And the soul that turneth after such as have familiar spirits… I will even set my face against that soul, and will cut him off from among his people."*
- *1 Samuel 28:7–8* – Saul sought out the medium of Endor to summon Samuel, an act of rebellion against God's clear command. The result was God's judgment and Saul's eventual downfall.

These passages reveal the grave danger of engaging with familiar spirits. What may seem to offer comfort, wisdom, or contact with the dead is, in reality, a deception that leads to spiritual bondage. The enemy uses these false encounters to lure people away from God's truth, fostering dependency on lies rather than reliance on the Holy Spirit. This bondage often manifests through fear, confusion, and a growing openness to deeper occult practices—all of which distance the soul from the freedom and guidance found only in Christ. Scripture warns us to avoid such practices entirely, seeking God alone as our ultimate source of truth and direction (Leviticus 19:31; Isaiah 8:19).

Strategies of Familiar Spirits

Familiar spirits are often described as targeting the mind by speaking in a "first-party" manner—presenting thoughts as though they originate from the individual. They specialize in imitation, deception, and the reinforcement of generational patterns, subtly influencing beliefs and behaviors through distorted internal dialogue. Their tactics include:

- *Mimicry of Loved Ones* – appearing in dreams, visions, or impressions as a deceased relative, offering counterfeit comfort. This exploits grief and keeps people bound to the past.
- *Reproducing Trauma* – reactivating old wounds by replaying memories, emotions, or circumstances that reinforce cycles of fear, rejection, or despair.
- *Emotional Manipulation* – feeding lies like "This pain will never end," "I'm cursed," "my family has always been this way," or "I'm worthless."
- *Counterfeit Spiritual Guidance* – posing as a guardian, guide, or even the Holy Spirit, but steering the person toward compromise and confusion.
- *Generational Bondage* – perpetuating cycles of sin such as rage, depression, witchcraft, addiction, or perversion, ensuring they pass down to future generations.

Common Entry Points

Familiar spirits gain legal access through various doors, often hidden or unrecognized:

- *Occult Involvement* – engaging in séances, psychic readings, astrology, witchcraft, tarot cards, or mediumship invites demonic impersonation.
- *Generational Idolatry or Covenants* – ancestral practices of false worship, witchcraft, Freemasonry, or bloodline pacts grant access that carries forward until renounced.
- *Trauma and Woundedness* – deep wounds, abuse, or grief can leave a soul vulnerable to counterfeit comfort or voices that appear familiar.
- *Unforgiveness and Bitterness* – unresolved anger or inner vows (e.g., "I'll never trust anyone again") create legal ground for spirits to remain.
- *Cultural or Religious Traditions* – rituals rooted in idolatry or spiritual compromise can open doors when practiced without discernment.

Effects of Familiar Spirits

When familiar spirits are active, their influence can be seen in:

- Persistent family cycles of addiction, rage, poverty, abuse, or mental torment.
- Supernatural manifestations (dreams, voices, visions) that imitate the dead or offer guidance.
- Counterfeit comfort that delays true healing and dependency on God.
- Entrenchment of generational strongholds that pass from parent to child.
- Resistance to spiritual growth due to confusion, false voices, or constant triggers.

Discernment is essential for every believer. The Holy Spirit gives us the wisdom to distinguish truth from deception and light from darkness. When we remain anchored in God's Word, filled with His Spirit, and submitted to His authority, the enemy's counterfeit voices lose their power. Familiar spirits may imitate truth, but they cannot produce the fruit of the Spirit or the peace of Christ. Freedom comes through intimacy with Jesus, obedience to His Word, and the continual renewing of the mind. In Him, every false light is exposed, and every chain is broken.

THE JEZEBEL SPIRIT

The Jezebel Spirit derives its name from Queen Jezebel in the Old Testament, one of the most notorious figures in Israel's history. As the wife of King Ahab of Israel, Jezebel introduced and institutionalized Baal worship, killed God's prophets, manipulated her husband, and persecuted God's servant Elijah. Her name has become synonymous with control, manipulation, and spiritual rebellion.

Jezebel in Scripture

- *1 Kings 18* – Jezebel orchestrated the murder of prophets and promoted Baal worship in Israel, standing in direct opposition to Elijah.
- *1 Kings 21* – She schemed Naboth's death to unlawfully seize his vineyard, demonstrating her use of false witnesses, intimidation, and manipulation for personal gain.
- *2 Kings 9* – Jezebel's death was as violent as her reign: she was thrown from a window, trampled by horses, and devoured by dogs, fulfilling Elijah's prophecy.

  "This is the word of the Lord that He spoke through His servant Elijah: 'On the plot of ground at Jezreel dogs will devour Jezebel's flesh.'" (2 Kings 9:36 NIV)

This historical account reveals the destructive power of the spirit that operated through Jezebel. Her influence did not end with her lifetime—the same manipulative, controlling, and deceitful spirit continues to operate in the world today, opposing godly authority and seeking to corrupt hearts away from truth.

CHARACTERISTICS OF THE JEZEBEL SPIRIT

- *Manipulation & Control* – Operates through schemes, deceit, and coercion. Jezebel manipulates circumstances and people to achieve selfish or destructive goals.
- *Resistance to Authority* – Refuses to submit to God's order, undermines godly leadership, and fosters rebellion.
- *False Prophecy & Deception* – Twists Scripture, introduces false teaching, and presents counterfeit spirituality to lead people astray.
- *Seduction & Immorality* – Encourages sexual immorality, unfaithfulness, and compromise with idolatry. This includes spiritual adultery — turning hearts away from God.
- *Intimidation & Fear* – Strikes fear into the hearts of God's servants. Elijah fled in fear after Jezebel threatened his life, despite just witnessing God's victory on Mount Carmel.

Manifestations

The Jezebel spirit is not confined to history. It continues to operate in subtle and overt ways today:

- *Undermines Leaders* – Seeks to discredit pastors, spiritual leaders, or anyone standing in God's authority.
- *Fosters Rebellion* – Stirs division in homes, churches, or ministries, especially against spiritual authority.
- *Infiltrates Churches* – Appears spiritual but spreads false teaching, divisive influence, or seduction. Revelation 2:20 warns of a "Jezebel" misleading the church at Thyatira into immorality and idolatry.

- *Manipulates Relationships* – Gains trust through charm or influence, then exerts control for personal or destructive agendas.
- *Promotes Compromise* – Encourages tolerance of sin, idolatry, and worldly values under the guise of "open-mindedness" or "spirituality."

THE PYTHON SPIRIT

The Python Spirit derives its name from Acts 16:16–18, where a slave girl in Philippi was possessed by a spirit of divination. In the original Greek, the term used is *pneuma pythōna*—literally meaning "a spirit of python." This referred to the mythological serpent associated with the oracle of Delphi in Greek culture, where fortune-telling and divination were practiced.

In Scripture, this spirit is revealed when Paul and Silas encounter the slave girl who followed them, proclaiming words that sounded true yet carried manipulation and distraction. Paul discerned the counterfeit nature of her message and, through the authority of Jesus Christ, commanded the spirit to depart—demonstrating the power of discernment and the supremacy of Christ over all spiritual deception.

> *"Once when we were going to the place of prayer, we were met by a female slave who had a spirit by which she predicted the future. She earned a great deal of money for her owners by fortune-telling. She followed Paul and the rest of us, shouting, 'These men are servants of the Most High God, who are telling you the way to be saved.' She kept this up for many days. Finally Paul became so annoyed that he turned around and said to the spirit, 'In the name of Jesus Christ I command you to come out of her!' At that moment the spirit left her." (Acts 16:16–18 NIV)*

Symbolism of the Python Spirit

The python is a constrictor snake, killing its prey by wrapping tightly around it until the breath is completely cut off. Spiritually, this mirrors the tactics of the Python Spirit—it seeks to constrict prayer, suffocate worship, and choke out spiritual vitality. Where the Spirit of God brings breath, life, and freedom, the python spirit attempts to drain strength, silence intercession, and sever intimacy with God. Its goal is to make believers spiritually exhausted, prayerless, and disconnected from the flow of the Holy Spirit—the very breath of God that sustains life.

Strategies of the Python Spirit

This spirit works subtly, often cloaked in religious or spiritual disguise:

- *Divination and Fortune-Telling* – Provides counterfeit revelation or insight apart from God, often mixed with partial truths to gain credibility.
- *Strangling Prayer Life* – Chokes out intercession, leaving believers feeling weary, distracted, or powerless in prayer.
- *Suffocating Worship* – Drains joy, passion, and freedom in worship, replacing it with heaviness or ritualism.
- *Counterfeit Prophecy* – Imitates the gifts of the Spirit, appearing spiritual but rooted in deception.
- *Oppression and Fatigue* – Creates an atmosphere of heaviness, exhaustion, and discouragement, making it difficult to press into God's presence.

Modern Manifestations

The python spirit often manifests in ways that undermine the spiritual vitality of individuals, families, or churches:

- Churches that experience constant division and prayerlessness.
- Leaders who feel drained or suffocated when trying to advance God's work.
- Individuals who experience constant spiritual fatigue or discouragement whenever they attempt to grow in prayer or worship.
- Movements where divination or counterfeit prophecy masquerades as Holy Spirit activity.

THE LEVIATHAN SPIRIT

The Leviathan Spirit is one of the most vividly described spiritual forces in Scripture, appearing in Job 41, Isaiah 27:1, and Psalm 74:13–14. Leviathan is pictured as a massive sea creature, fierce, untamable, and terrifying. While the literal image is of a dragon-like serpent, biblically and symbolically it represents pride, chaos, rebellion, and confusion.

Leviathan in Scripture

- *Job 41* – Entirely dedicated to describing Leviathan: impenetrable armor, fire-breathing, overwhelming strength, and a creature that no man can subdue. Job's description portrays Leviathan as unstoppable by human power.
Isaiah 27:1 (KJV) – *"In that day the Lord with his sore and great and strong sword shall punish leviathan the piercing serpent, even leviathan that crooked serpent; and he shall slay the dragon that is in the sea."*
Psalm 74:13–14 (NIV) – *"It was you who split open the sea by your power; you broke the heads of the monster in the waters. It was you who crushed the heads of Leviathan and gave it as food to the creatures of the desert."*

These passages remind us that although Leviathan is fierce, God alone has the power to defeat him.

Attributes of Leviathan (Job 41 imagery)

- *Armor-like Scales* – Symbolizes hardened pride, an unteachable and impenetrable heart.
- *Fire-Breathing Imagery* – Symbolizes destructive words, intimidation, and arrogant defiance.
- *Unstoppable Force* – Represents rebellion that resists peace, unity, and submission to God.
- *Twisted and Coiled* – The very name "Leviathan" comes from the Hebrew *livyathan*, meaning "to twist or coil," representing distortion, perversion, and confusion.

Strategies of the Leviathan Spirit

- *Division* – Leviathan thrives on creating strife in relationships, families, churches, and communities.
- *Covenant-Breaking* – Works to destroy marriages, leadership covenants, and sacred agreements.
- *Confusion in Relationships* – Twists words, misrepresents intentions, and fosters misunderstanding.
- *Manipulation* – Uses pride and deception to turn people against one another.
- *Resistance to Peace* – Prevents reconciliation and inflames quarrels, keeping people in chaos.

"For where envying and strife is, there is confusion and every evil work." (James 3:16)

MANIFESTATIONS

Leviathan is often behind chronic relational dysfunction and spiritual unrest:

- Marriages constantly battling strife and miscommunication.
- Churches plagued by division, gossip, and pride.
- Individuals' resistant to correction, consumed by self-righteousness,
- Communities or families where confusion always surrounds critical decisions.
- Leaders who fall to arrogance, destroying unity and integrity.

Awareness involves more than simply acknowledging that a spiritual problem exists; it requires cultivating a posture of discernment—understanding the enemy's strategies of deception, the power of belief, and the necessity of putting on God's armor. True discernment allows us to see beyond the surface of our struggles and recognize the spiritual forces operating behind them.

No one seeks a solution for a problem they can't see or don't believe exists; therefore, awareness of a deeper problem is the first step toward change. Without it, people remain trapped in cycles of confusion, deception, and defeat. But once the enemy's schemes are exposed, his power begins to crumble. Only when we are able to see beneath the surface can we reach the real problem. We must understand what is causing the manifestation. Jesus, the Light of the world, shines truth into every dark place—exposing the tactics of the adversary and revealing the divine authority we possess in Him.

Still, awareness alone is not the final step. Recognizing the battle is only the beginning; we must also engage it. True freedom comes when awareness is followed by repentance, prayer, deliverance and ongoing discipleship. Awareness provides clarity, prayer establishes connection with God, deliverance brings breakthrough through His power and discipleship helps us build a strong relationship with Jesus. It's a lifelong journey of transformation—step by step, day by day—where Jesus rescues us, trains us, corrects us, heals us, and sends us out to join Him in His work.

As our awareness grows, we are being prepared for the greater work of deliverance. Our spiritual eyes open to see the strongholds that must be torn down, the lies that must be renounced, and the spirits that must be cast out or cast away in the name of Jesus. Awareness is not the destination—it is part of preparation. It positions us to move into the next vital dimension: the power of prayer and deliverance.

Dealing with the everyday common Minion Spirits

- Desire and sexual temptation
- Lust
- Pornography / perversion
- Adultery / unfaithfulness
- Seduction
- Fantasy / impurity
- Compulsion / addiction (sexual or otherwise)

Fear and anxiety

- Fear
- Worry / anxiety
- Panic
- Intimidation
- Terror / dread
- Control (fear-driven)

Mind and emotions

- Depression / heaviness
- Despair / hopelessness
- Rejection

- Orphan mindset (abandonment / insecurity)
- Shame / condemnation
- Confusion
- Double-mindedness

Anger and relational destruction

- Anger / rage
- Offense
- Bitterness
- Unforgiveness
- Hatred
- Strife / contention
- Division (in homes, churches, friendships)

Pride and self-exaltation

- Pride
- Arrogance
- Self-righteousness / religious spirit
- Independence (refusing counsel / accountability)
- Boasting / vanity

Deception and compromise

- Lying
- Deception
- Manipulation
- False accusation
- Gossip / slander
- Jezebel-like control (control, seduction, domination— used carefully)
- Delilah-like compromise (weakening boundaries)

Bondage and compulsions

- Addiction (substances, food, gambling, screens, etc.)
- Gluttony
- Sloth / apathy
- Escapism
- Compulsion (repetitive sin cycles)

Infirmity and affliction

- Infirmity (physical affliction, chronic weakness—often discussed alongside wisdom and medical care)
- Insomnia / tormenting restlessness
- Self-harm / self-destruction (high-stakes—handle with care)
- Suicidal oppression (high-stakes—needs immediate support if present)

Occult and counterfeit spirituality

- Occult involvement / witchcraft
- Divination
- Sorcery
- New Age deception
- Idolatry (anything replacing God as source)

Chapter 9
FILLED & EMPOWERED

"May God himself, the God of peace, sanctify you through and through. May your whole spirit, soul and body be kept blameless at the coming of our Lord Jesus Christ." — 1 Thessalonians 5:23 (NIV)

Freedom from oppression is not God's final purpose. He does not simply cleanse His people so they can live relieved lives; He cleanses them so they can become dwelling places of His presence. A temple is not made holy merely by what is removed from it, but by who fills it.

In the same way, deliverance is not complete when darkness leaves—it is complete when the Holy Spirit fully occupies what has been reclaimed for God. The ultimate purpose of cleansing the temple is not merely freedom but fullness—being filled with the Holy Spirit, anointed and empowered for God's purposes. Cleansing without filling leaves a dangerous void, and an unfilled space can become an open invitation for the enemy's return. Paul reminds believers,

"Your bodies are temples of the Holy Spirit, who is in you, whom you have received from God. You are not your own" *(1 Corinthians 6:19).*

A cleansed temple is never meant to remain empty; it is meant to become the dwelling place of the Holy Spirit, the living God. Jesus warned that when a house is swept clean but left unoccupied, the spirits that once departed may return—bringing even more evil spirits with them and seeking to reclaim what was once theirs. True deliverance, therefore, is not completed simply by removing darkness, but by filling the cleansed space with the presence, power, and rule of the Holy Spirit.

> *"When an impure spirit comes out of a person, it goes through arid places seeking rest and does not find it. Then it says, 'I will return to the house I left.' When it arrives, it finds the house unoccupied, swept clean and put in order. Then it goes and takes with it seven other spirits more wicked than itself, and they go in and live there. And the final condition of that person is worse than the first. That is how it will be with this wicked generation." (Matthew 12:43–45 NIV).*

THE BRIDE MADE READY

Cleansing serves an eternal purpose: preparing the Bride of Christ. The work God does through deliverance, healing, and sanctification is never limited to personal relief alone; it is part of His greater work of preparing His people for Himself. Jesus is actively sanctifying His Church, cleansing and restoring her so that she may stand before Him radiant, pure, and whole.

> *"and to present her to himself as a radiant church, without stain or wrinkle or any other blemish, but holy and blameless." (Ephesians 5:27 NIV)*

Every stronghold torn down, every curse broken, every wound healed, and every lie replaced with truth moves the Bride closer to her destiny. What God restores in individual lives contributes to what He is preparing corporately in His Church. Our personal freedom therefore becomes part of the larger redemptive work through which Christ is preparing His people for the day of His return.

Scripture gives us a glimpse of that coming fulfillment in the marriage supper of the Lamb:

> *"Let us rejoice and be glad and give him glory! For the wedding of the Lamb has come, and his bride has made herself ready. Fine linen, bright and clean, was given her to wear… Then the angel said to me, 'Write this: Blessed are those who are invited to the wedding supper of the Lamb!'" (Revelation 19:7–9 NIV)*

Cleansing therefore is not only about freedom from bondage; it is also about readiness for union, holiness, and eternal belonging. As Christ heals, purifies, and restores His people, He is preparing a Bride who reflects His beauty, bears His character, and is ready for His appearing. The freedom God gives today is part of the preparation for the glory that is to come.

LIVING A SPIRIT-FILLED LIFESTYLE

Living as a temple of the Holy Spirit means allowing God's presence to fill and guide every area of life. When the Spirit dwells within the believer, His presence brings light, truth, and power into the places that were once shaped by fear, bondage, and deception. What once belonged to darkness is gradually replaced with peace, wisdom, and spiritual authority.

The Holy Spirit does not merely visit the believer—He dwells within, shaping the life of the one who welcomes His leadership and responds to His guidance.

Scripture reminds us of this profound reality:

> *"Do you not know that your bodies are temples of the Holy Spirit, who is in you, whom you have received from God?" (1 Corinthians 6:19 NIV)*

To live as a temple of the Holy Spirit means allowing His presence to guide our thoughts, direct our choices, and shape our character. As His Spirit fills the believer, darkness loses its place, and the life of Christ begins to be expressed more clearly through us.

A Spirit-filled life is therefore not a single moment of encounter but an ongoing posture of surrender. Each day the believer chooses to welcome the Holy Spirit's influence—allowing Him to lead, correct, comfort, and empower.

Paul encourages believers to live continually under the influence of the Spirit when he writes:

> *"Do not get drunk on wine, which leads to debauchery. Instead, be filled with the Spirit."(Ephesians 5:18 NIV)*

The language of this passage implies a continual filling—a life that repeatedly turns toward the presence of God. As believers yield themselves to the Spirit, He fills the temple again and again, strengthening them to live in truth, holiness, and freedom.

In this way, the temple remains occupied by the life of God Himself, leaving no room for darkness to return. A Spirit-filled life is cultivated through daily practices that keep the heart attentive to the presence and leading of the Holy Spirit.

This includes:

- **Daily Intimacy with Jesus**
Abiding in His presence and remaining connected to the true source of life.

"Remain in me, as I also remain in you. No branch can bear fruit by itself; it must remain in the vine. Neither can you bear fruit unless you remain in me.

'I am the vine; you are the branches. If you remain in me and I in you, you will bear much fruit; apart from me you can do nothing.'"(John 15:4–5 NIV)

- **Walking in the Spirit**

Allowing the Holy Spirit to guide our thoughts, decisions, and actions.

> *"So I say, walk by the Spirit, and you will not gratify the desires of the flesh."(Galatians 5:16 NIV)*

> *"Since we live by the Spirit, let us keep in step with the Spirit." (Galatians 5:25 NIV)*

- **Quick, honest repentance and regular forgiveness**

Keeping the heart clear, humble, and responsive to God.

> *"If we confess our sins, he is faithful and just and will forgive us our sins and purify us from all unrighteousness." (1 John 1:9 NIV)*

> *"For if you forgive other people when they sin against you, your heavenly Father will also forgive you." (Matthew 6:14 NIV)*

- **Staying anchored in the Word**

Allowing God's truth to renew the mind and shape our thinking.

> *"Do not conform to the pattern of this world, but be transformed by the renewing of your mind."*

(Romans 12:2 NIV)

"Your word is a lamp for my feet, a light on my path."
(Psalm 119:105 NIV)

- **Healthy community and accountability**

Remaining connected to the body of Christ for encourage
ment, wisdom, and correction.

"And let us consider how we may spur one another on to-
ward love and good deeds, not giving up meeting together…
but encouraging one another." (Hebrews 10:24–25 NIV)

"As iron sharpens iron, so one person sharpens another."
(Proverbs 27:17 NIV)

God never designed the Christian life to be lived in isolation. Freedom and spiritual growth are strengthened through
fellowship with other believers who walk together in faith.
Within the body of Christ we find encouragement, wisdom,
accountability, and loving correction. Through this shared life
in Christ, believers are strengthened to continue walking in the
light and living as temples of the Holy Spirit.

MAINTAINING THE GIFT OF FREEDOM

Deliverance marks the beginning of a new way of life, not
the end of a process. Freedom is sustained as believers remain
closely connected to the One who set them free. Continued
time in the presence of Christ brings ongoing renewal and transformation, strengthening the believer to walk in lasting freedom.

Part of stewarding that freedom involves guarding the areas
through which influence enters the heart.

Guarding the Gates

Scripture teaches that the enemy often seeks to regain influence through unguarded gateways in a person's life. These gateways are not only physical senses but spiritual entry points through which ideas, temptations, and influences shape the inner life.

Because the believer has been cleansed and filled with the Holy Spirit, these gates must now be stewarded with wisdom and discernment.

These gateways include:

- **Eyes** — what we choose to watch, observe, and dwell upon. The things we repeatedly look at often shape our desires and thoughts. Scripture warns believers to be mindful of what they set before their eyes.

"I will set before my eyes no vile thing."(Psalm 101:3 NIV)

- **Ears** — the voices and messages we allow to influence us. Words have power to shape beliefs and direct the heart. Listening to truth strengthens faith, while listening to deception can distort it.

"Consequently, faith comes from hearing the message, and the message is heard through the word about Christ." (Romans 10:17 NIV)

- **Mind** — the thoughts we entertain or dismiss. The mind is one of the primary battlefields in spiritual warfare. Believers are called not merely to observe thoughts but to bring them into submission to Christ.

"We take captive every thought to make it obedient to Christ." (2 Corinthians 10:5 NIV)

- **Heart** — the motives, desires, and affections we nurture within. The heart is the center of spiritual life, where decisions and loyalties are formed. What is cultivated there eventually directs the course of life.

"Above all else, guard your heart, for everything you do flows from it." (Proverbs 4:23 NIV)

Because these gateways influence the inner life, believers are called to remain spiritually attentive. Guarding the gates does not mean living in fear or suspicion; rather, it means living with awareness and discernment, allowing the Holy Spirit to guide what we allow into our thoughts and affections.

Peter reminds believers of the importance of this vigilance:

"Be alert and of sober mind. Your enemy the devil prowls around like a roaring lion looking for someone to devour." (1 Peter 5:8 NIV)

Paul echoes the same warning, encouraging believers to close any opportunity the enemy might use to regain influence:

"Do not let the sun go down while you are still angry, and do not give the devil a foothold." (Ephesians 4:26–27 NIV)

Guarding the gates therefore involves intentional spiritual practices. When the Holy Spirit brings conviction, believers respond quickly through repentance. When temptations arise, they reject them and replace them with truth. When wounds or offenses appear, forgiveness closes the door to bitterness and prevents the enemy from gaining ground.

Accountability within the body of Christ also strengthens this process. Trusted brothers and sisters help bring clarity, encouragement, and correction when blind spots appear. Together, believers help safeguard one another's hearts as they walk in freedom.

Yet guarding the gates of our lives requires more than vigilance; it requires a humble and teachable heart before God. A life that remains open to the work of the Holy Spirit continues to grow, mature, and deepen in spiritual understanding.

HUMILITY AND GROWTH

Spiritual life is never static. We are either progressing or regressing, advancing or drifting—there is no standing still in the life of faith. Humility keeps the heart soft, teachable, and pliable before God (Matthew 5:3; 1 Peter 5:5–6). The Holy Spirit is always ready to teach and lead us into truth; our responsibility is to remain humble, willing, and ready to learn.

"In the same way, you who are younger, submit yourselves to your elders. All of you, clothe yourselves with humility toward one another, because, "God opposes the proud but shows favor to the humble." Humble yourselves, therefore, under God's mighty hand, that he may lift you up in due time." (1 Peter 5:5–6 NIV)

DAILY SURRENDER

Humility ultimately leads the believer into a life of surrender. A heart that remains humble before God becomes willing to yield every area of life to His leadership. Surrender is not a single moment of decision but a continual posture of the heart—an ongoing willingness to allow the Holy Spirit to shape our desires, direct our choices, and transform our character.

Deliverance may remove what once bound us, but surrender allows the new life of Christ to grow within us. As believers place their lives before the Lord each day—offering their thoughts, desires, plans, and decisions to Him—they learn that true spiritual strength is not found in striving but in yielding to the work of the Spirit.

Scripture describes this posture as offering ourselves to God as a living sacrifice. Rather than attempting to control our own lives, we entrust them to the leadership of the Holy Spirit, allowing Him to guide, correct, and strengthen us as we walk with Christ. In this way, the freedom Christ has given continues to mature and deepen over time.

The Bible describes this surrendered life in these powerful words:

> *"I have been crucified with Christ and I no longer live, but Christ lives in me. The life I now live in the body, I live by faith in the Son of God, who loved me and gave himself for me." (Galatians 2:20 NIV)*

When believers live in this posture of surrender, Christ's life becomes increasingly visible through them. His love replaces selfish ambition, His wisdom guides our decisions, and His strength empowers us to walk in obedience. Day by day, the believer learns that the Christian life is not about trying harder to follow Christ—it is about allowing Christ Himself to live through us.

THE ANOINTING OF THE HOLY SPIRIT

When a life is surrendered to God and filled with His Spirit, Scripture describes the work of the Holy Spirit as an anointing. Throughout the Bible, anointing represents God setting someone apart and empowering them for His purposes.

In the Old Testament, oil was often used as a visible symbol of this spiritual reality. Kings, priests, and prophets were anointed as a sign that God had chosen them and placed His Spirit upon them to accomplish His work.

When the prophet Samuel anointed David, Scripture records:

> *"So Samuel took the horn of oil and anointed him in the presence of his brothers, and from that day on the Spir-*

it of the LORD came powerfully upon David."(1 Samuel 16:13 NIV)

The oil itself did not carry the power. It served as a symbol pointing to the greater reality—the Spirit of God empowering the person whom He had chosen.

Throughout Scripture, anointing with oil reflects several important spiritual truths:

- **Consecration** — being set apart for God's purposes (Exodus 30:30; 1 Samuel 16:13)

- **Healing** — God's restoring work in the lives of His people
  "Is anyone among you sick? Let them call the elders of the church to pray over them and anoint them with oil in the name of the Lord."
  (James 5:14–15 NIV)

- **Joy and blessing** — the refreshing presence of God upon His people
  "You have loved righteousness and hated wickedness; therefore God, your God, has set you above your companions by anointing you with the oil of joy." (Psalm 45:7 NIV)

Yet Scripture makes clear that the power is not in the oil itself. Oil simply points to the work of the Holy Spirit, who alone consecrates, heals, and empowers believers for the work of God.

Jesus Himself described His ministry in these terms:

"The Spirit of the Lord is on me, because he has anointed me to proclaim good news to the poor." (Luke 4:18 NIV)

For believers today, the anointing is not primarily a ceremony but a spiritual reality. When the Holy Spirit fills a life that has been cleansed and surrendered to God, He empowers that person to walk in truth, minister to others, and carry the presence of Christ into the world.

In this way, the temple that has been cleansed and filled becomes a place where the Spirit of God not only dwells but also moves through the believer to bring healing, truth, and freedom to others.

Yet Scripture consistently reminds us that the power is not in the oil itself. Oil simply points to the work of the Holy Spirit, who alone consecrates, heals, and empowers believers for the work of God.

Jesus Himself declared that His ministry flowed from this anointing:

> *"The Spirit of the Lord is on me, because he has anointed me to proclaim good news to the poor." (Luke 4:18 NIV)*

For the believer today, the anointing is not primarily a ceremony but a spiritual reality. When the Holy Spirit fills a life that has been cleansed and surrendered to God, He empowers that person to walk in truth, minister to others, and carry the presence of Christ into the world.

In this way, the temple that has been cleansed and filled becomes a place where the Spirit of God not only dwells but also moves through the believer to bring healing, truth, and freedom to others.

TRANSFORMATION: BECOMING LIKE THE SOLUTION

When the temple of a believer's life has been cleansed and filled with the Holy Spirit, the work of God does not stop there.

Deliverance opens the door to freedom, but the life that follows becomes an ongoing process of transformation. The Spirit who fills the temple now begins shaping the life of the believer from the inside out.

Christian transformation is not merely behavior modification or religious effort—it is the work of the Holy Spirit renewing the heart, mind, and character of the believer. As we remain in God's presence, His Spirit reshapes our desires, purifies our motives, and aligns our lives with His truth.

Scripture describes this transformation as a renewal that unfolds as we walk with Him:

> *"Do not conform to the pattern of this world, but be transformed by the renewing of your mind."(Romans 12:2 NIV)*

The word *transformed* describes a deep inner change—a spiritual metamorphosis that takes place as believers encounter God through His Word, prayer, and the work of the Holy Spirit within them.

Paul describes this process in these words:

> *"And we all, who with unveiled faces contemplate the Lord's glory, are being transformed into his image with ever-increasing glory, which comes from the Lord, who is the Spirit." (2 Corinthians 3:18 NIV)*

As we remain in His presence, the Spirit reshapes our thoughts, desires, and identity until Christ is increasingly formed within us.

> *"My dear children, for whom I am again in the pains of childbirth until Christ is formed in you." (Galatians 4:19 NIV)*

Transformation is therefore not a single moment but a life-long journey. Day by day the Holy Spirit refines us, teaches us, corrects us, and strengthens us so that the life of Christ becomes increasingly visible in us.

The temple that has been cleansed and filled becomes a place where the presence of God is revealed to the world.

THE PURPOSE OF CLEANSING

Cleansing the temple was never meant to be the end of the story. Freedom is the doorway into a life that reflects the presence, character, and power of Christ.

When Jesus cleanses a life, He does so with the intention of filling it with His Spirit. When the Spirit fills the temple, transformation begins. And as transformation unfolds, the believer becomes a living testimony of God's redeeming work.

The life that was once burdened by darkness becomes a dwelling place of light. The heart that was once captive becomes a vessel through which God's presence flows to others.

- Freedom leads to transformation.
- Transformation prepares the believer for service.
- And a life surrendered to the Holy Spirit becomes a testimony of the redeeming power of Christ.

This is the ultimate purpose of cleansing—not merely relief from oppression, but restoration into the life God originally intended. The temple that has been cleansed and filled becomes a place where the presence of God dwells and where His work continues through the life of the believer.

Reflection Questions

Take a few moments to sit quietly with the Lord and reflect on the work He may be doing in your life.

1. Are there areas of my life where the Holy Spirit is inviting deeper cleansing or surrender?
2. Do I truly see my life as a temple of the Holy Spirit? How might that understanding change the way I live, think, or respond to challenges?
3. Are there gates in my life—what I watch, listen to, or dwell upon—that need greater guarding and discernment?
4. Am I cultivating daily intimacy with Jesus, or have other priorities begun to crowd out time in His presence?
5. In what ways is the Holy Spirit currently transforming my heart, thoughts, or character?
6. What would it look like for me to surrender more fully to the leadership of the Holy Spirit in my daily life?

Take time to bring these questions before the Lord in prayer. Allow the Holy Spirit to gently reveal areas where He is continuing His work of cleansing, filling, and transforming your life.

Prayer
Lord Jesus

Thank You for the freedom You purchased through Your sacrifice. Thank You for cleansing my life and breaking the power of darkness over me.

Today I surrender my heart to You again. Search every part of my life and reveal anything that does not belong to You. I choose to turn from every lie, every foothold, and every agreement with the enemy.

Holy Spirit, fill every part of my life. Guide my thoughts, guard my heart, and lead me in truth. Teach me to walk daily in humility, surrender, and obedience to You. Let my life become a temple where Your presence dwells and Your light shines.

In Jesus' name, Amen.

DECLARATION OF FREEDOM

In the name of Jesus Christ, I declare:

- **I am a temple of the Holy Spirit, redeemed and set apart for God's glory.**
  "Do you not know that your bodies are temples of the Holy Spirit, who is in you, whom you have received from God? You are not your own; you were bought at a price. Therefore honor God with your bodies." (1 Corinthians 6:19–20 NIV)

- **I have been rescued from the dominion of darkness and brought into the kingdom of Christ.**
  "For he has rescued us from the dominion of darkness and brought us into the kingdom of the Son he loves." (Colossians 1:13 NIV)

- **Through Jesus Christ, I am free from every curse and every claim of the enemy.**
  "Christ redeemed us from the curse of the law by becoming a curse for us, for it is written: 'Cursed is everyone who is hung on a pole.'" (Galatians 3:13 NIV)

- **The Spirit of God lives within me and empowers me to walk in truth and freedom.**
  "But you will receive power when the Holy Spirit comes on you; and you will be my witnesses in Jerusalem, and in all Judea and Samaria, and to the ends of the earth." (Acts 1:8 NIV)

- **I will stand firm in the freedom Christ has given me.**
  "It is for freedom that Christ has set us free. Stand firm, then, and do not let yourselves be burdened again by a yoke of slavery."
  (Galatians 5:1 NIV)

- **Christ is forming His life within me.**
  "My dear children, for whom I am again in the pains of childbirth until Christ is formed in you." (Galatians 4:19 NIV)

- **I am part of the radiant Bride of Christ being prepared for His return.**
  "and to present her to himself as a radiant church, without stain or wrinkle or any other blemish, but holy and blameless." (Ephesians 5:27 NIV)

The temple that Christ has cleansed and filled now belongs fully to Him, and His Spirit continues the work of transformation until the day we stand before Him in glory.(Ephesians 5:27)

Chapter 10
PRAYER & MEDITATION

"Let us then approach God's throne of grace with confidence, so that we may receive mercy and find grace to help us in our time of need." (Hebrews 4:16 NIV)

Freedom in Christ is not sustained through a single moment of victory but through an ongoing relationship with the One who set us free. Deliverance may remove what once held influence over our lives, but continued freedom is strengthened through daily communion with God.

Scripture repeatedly calls believers to remain connected to the Lord, not only in moments of crisis or need but as a continual posture of the heart. Jesus described this relationship using the image of a vine and its branches:

"Remain in me, as I also remain in you. No branch can bear fruit by itself; it must remain in the vine. Neither can you bear fruit unless you remain in me." (John 15:4 NIV)

Just as a branch receives life from the vine, believers receive spiritual life, strength, and discernment through abiding in Christ. When this connection remains strong, the life of God continues to flow through the believer, strengthening the heart against deception and reinforcing the freedom that Christ has given.

One of the primary ways believers cultivate this abiding relationship is through prayer and meditation on Scripture. These practices are not merely religious disciplines but invitations into an active and living communion with God. Through prayer we speak with God, bringing our praise, confession, gratitude, and needs before Him. Through meditation we quiet our hearts, reflect on His Word, and allow His truth to reshape our thinking.

Throughout Scripture, prayer and meditation appear together as complementary practices that draw believers into deeper fellowship with the Lord. Prayer allows the believer to express the heart toward God, while meditation creates space to reflect on His truth and receive His guidance.

Together these practices form a pattern of spiritual life—speaking with God and listening to Him.

As prayer and meditation become part of daily life, believers grow in spiritual awareness and discernment. They learn to recognize the leading of the Holy Spirit and to walk in step with Him rather than drifting back into patterns that once led to bondage.

In this way, prayer and meditation serve not only as practices of devotion but as essential safeguards for spiritual freedom. They help ensure that the temple God has cleansed remains filled with His presence and aligned with His truth.

THE POWER OF PRAYER

The Lord calls every believer to partner with Him in advancing His Kingdom within a broken and dying world. Through our petitions, intercession, and alignment with His will—joined with His divine power—His purposes are released and carried out on earth. Jesus made this truth unmistakably clear when He emphasized both the authority and the sacred responsibility He has entrusted to His followers.

"Whatever you bind on earth will be bound in heaven, and whatever you loose on earth will be loosed in heaven." (Matthew 18:18 NIV)

Effective prayer operates under divine principles established by God. We have access to the Father through Jesus Christ, who serves as the mediator between God and mankind.

"For there is one God and one mediator between God and mankind, the man Christ Jesus."(1 Timothy 2:5 NIV)

The power of prayer is also made possible through the Holy Spirit, who intercedes for us when we are weak and uncertain of how to pray. He gives voice to the deep cries of our hearts—those that words cannot express.

"In the same way, the Spirit helps us in our weakness. We do not know what we ought to pray for, but the Spirit himself intercedes for us through wordless groans. And he who searches our hearts knows the mind of the Spirit, because the Spirit intercedes for God's people in accordance with the will of God." (Romans 8:26–27 NIV)

Prayer requires alignment with God's truth, His Word, and His character, ensuring that our requests flow from His revealed will and eternal purposes rather than from personal impulse or preference.

"If you remain in me and my words remain in you, ask whatever you wish, and it will be done for you." (John 15:7 NIV)

Scripture reminds us that prayer offered from a heart aligned with God carries powerful influence.

"Therefore confess your sins to each other and pray for each other so that you may be healed. The prayer of a righteous person is powerful and effective." (James 5:16 NIV)

True prayer must be rooted in faith, not doubt—trusting that God hears and responds according to His perfect will. Praying in His name means far more than simply concluding a prayer with the words "in Jesus' name." It is to pray in alignment with His character, according to His will, under His authority, and with complete trust in His finished work.

Believers are called to pray with authority in the name of Jesus—representing His will and relying on the power He provides rather than their own.

"And I will do whatever you ask in my name, so that the Father may be glorified in the Son. You may ask me for anything in my name, and I will do it." (John 14:13–14 NIV)

"Very truly I tell you, my Father will give you whatever you ask in my name…" (John 16:23–24 NIV)

WHAT PRAYER PRODUCES IN THE LIFE OF THE BELIEVER

Through prayer, believers experience transformation in several important ways.

1. Building a Personal Relationship with Jesus

Prayer deepens our relationship with the Lord. As we spend time in His presence, He transforms us into His likeness. Jesus not only desires a relationship with His followers but actively pursues, knows, and cares for them personally.

*"Come near to God and he will come near to you."
(James 4:8 NIV)*

"And we all, who with unveiled faces contemplate the Lord's glory, are being transformed into his image with ever-increasing glory." (2 Corinthians 3:18 NIV)

2. Receiving Spiritual Wisdom and Guidance

Spiritual wisdom is not the same as worldly wisdom. True wisdom comes "from above," originating in God rather than human reasoning. It is rooted in reverence for the Lord and guided by the Holy Spirit.

"If any of you lacks wisdom, you should ask God, who gives generously to all without finding fault." (James 1:5 NIV)

Worldly wisdom, by contrast, is driven by self-interest and shaped apart from dependence on God.

"Such 'wisdom' does not come down from heaven but is earthly, unspiritual, demonic... But the wisdom that comes from heaven is first of all pure; then peace-loving, considerate, submissive, full of mercy and good fruit." (James 3:13–17 NIV)

3. Experiencing Peace Beyond Understanding

Prayer also brings supernatural peace into situations that might otherwise produce fear or anxiety.

"Do not be anxious about anything, but in every situation, by prayer and petition, with thanksgiving, present your requests to God. And the peace of God... will guard your hearts and your minds in Christ Jesus." (Philippians 4:6–7 NIV)

4. Inviting Divine Intervention

Prayer invites God's involvement in human circumstances. Divine intervention occurs when the natural order is interrupted by the supernatural power of God.

> *"Ask and it will be given to you; seek and you will find; knock and the door will be opened to you. (Matthew 7:7–8 NIV)*

5. Engaging in Spiritual Warfare

Prayer is also a vital part of spiritual warfare. Believers stand firm against the enemy through dependence upon God and the authority of Christ.

> *"And pray in the Spirit on all occasions with all kinds of prayers and requests." (Ephesians 6:18 NIV)*

6. Interceding for Others

Intercession is a vital component of fulfilling the Great Commission. When believers intercede, they stand before God on behalf of others, praying that His redemptive purposes would be accomplished in their lives.

> *"I urge, then, first of all, that petitions, prayers, intercession and thanksgiving be made for all people." (1 Timothy 2:1 NIV)*

THE MANY EXPRESSIONS OF PRAYER

Prayer in Scripture is multifaceted. It is not limited to a single form but reflects an active and living relationship with God expressed in several different ways. Throughout the Bible we see believers approaching the Lord through worship, repentance, gratitude, requests, and intercession.

These expressions of prayer help believers engage with God honestly and fully. While the specific categories can help us understand how prayer functions, the most important aspect is the heart behind it—bringing every need, concern, and praise before the Lord in faith and sincerity.

Adoration – Worship and Praise for Who God Is

Adoration focuses entirely on honoring God for His character. In this expression of prayer we acknowledge His holiness, greatness, and authority as Creator and Lord. Rather than asking for anything, adoration centers the heart on worship, reverence, and gratitude.

When believers worship God in prayer, their perspective begins to shift. Problems and circumstances no longer dominate the center of attention—God does. Adoration reminds us that the One we are speaking to is sovereign over all things.

"Come, let us bow down in worship, let us kneel before the Lord our Maker." (Psalm 95:6 NIV)

Confession – Acknowledging Sin and Receiving Forgiveness

Confession is the humble act of acknowledging sin before the Lord. It is not about condemnation but restoration. God invites His people to approach Him honestly, recognizing where they have fallen short and receiving the forgiveness He freely offers.

Confession keeps the heart soft before God and prevents hidden sin from creating distance in our relationship with Him. Through confession we experience cleansing, renewal, and restored fellowship.

"If we confess our sins, he is faithful and just and will forgive us our sins and purify us from all unrighteousness." (1 John 1:9 NIV

Thanksgiving – Gratitude for God's Blessings

Thanksgiving expresses gratitude for what God has already done. It acknowledges His faithfulness, provision, and mercy in our lives.

Even in difficult circumstances, thanksgiving reminds us that God is still present and still working. A grateful heart strengthens faith and shifts our focus away from fear toward trust in His goodness.

"Give thanks in all circumstances; for this is God's will for you in Christ Jesus." (1 Thessalonians 5:18 NIV)

Supplication – Presenting Personal Requests to God

Supplication refers to bringing our personal needs before the Lord. It involves asking God for guidance, provision, wisdom, or intervention.

Supplication reflects our dependence upon Him. Rather than carrying life's burdens alone, we place them in the hands of the One who is able to sustain and provide.

"Do not be anxious about anything, but in every situation, by prayer and petition, with thanksgiving, present your requests to God." (Philippians 4:6 NIV)

Intercession – Praying on Behalf of Others

Intercession involves standing before God on behalf of another person. Jesus Himself models this ministry, continually interceding for His followers.

Through intercession believers carry the needs and struggles of others into the presence of God. In this way, intercession becomes a sacred partnership with God's redemptive purposes.

> *"I urge, then, first of all, that petitions, prayers, intercession and thanksgiving be made for all people." (1 Timothy 2:1 NIV)*

> *"I looked for someone among them who would build up the wall and stand before me in the gap on behalf of the land…"(Ezekiel 22:30 NIV)*

Healing – Praying for the Sick

Healing prayer invites God's restoring power into situations of sickness, pain, and suffering. Throughout Scripture God reveals Himself as *Jehovah Rapha*—the Lord who heals.

Believers are encouraged to pray for the sick, trusting in God's compassion and authority over the human body.

> *"The prayer of a righteous person is powerful and effective."* *(James 5:16 NIV)*

> *"Praise the Lord… who forgives all your sins and heals all your diseases." (Psalm 103:2–3 NIV)*

> *"By his wounds we are healed." (Isaiah 53:5 NIV)*

Deliverance and Spiritual Warfare

Prayer also functions as a place of spiritual authority. Believers live within a spiritual conflict where the enemy seeks to deceive and oppress. Through prayer we stand in the authority of Christ and resist the influence of darkness.

Deliverance and spiritual warfare prayer rely not on human strength but on the authority of Jesus and the power of the Holy Spirit.

> *"The weapons we fight with are not the weapons of the world... they have divine power to demolish strongholds."* *(2 Corinthians 10:4 NIV)*

> *"Pray in the Spirit on all occasions with all kinds of prayers and requests." (Ephesians 6:18 NIV)*

> *"Whatever you bind on earth will be bound in heaven..." (Matthew 18:18 NIV)*

Corporate Prayer – The Power of Believers Praying Together

While personal prayer builds intimacy with God, corporate prayer strengthens unity within the body of Christ. When believers gather together in prayer, their faith joins in agreement and their voices rise together before the Lord.

Throughout Scripture, corporate prayer is often connected with revival, breakthrough, and spiritual awakening.

> *"For where two or three gather in my name, there am I with them." (Matthew 18:20 NIV)*

MEDITATION ON SCRIPTURE

While prayer allows believers to speak with God, meditation invites the believer to slow down and reflect upon His Word, allowing His truth to shape the heart and mind. Prayer expresses the heart toward God, while meditation creates space for the believer to listen, consider, and absorb the wisdom God reveals through Scripture.

In Scripture, meditation does not mean emptying the mind. Instead, it means filling the mind with the truth of God and intentionally reflecting upon His Word. Through meditation, believers allow Scripture to move beyond intellectual understanding and take root within the heart, gradually transforming thoughts, attitudes, and desires.

Every sheep eventually learns to recognize the voice of the Shepherd. As they spend time with Him, they begin to discern His tone, His leading, and His truth. A sheep that belongs to the Shepherd grows familiar with His voice and will not follow a stranger, because relationship produces recognition. The more time believers spend with the Lord, the more clearly they begin to recognize His guidance and His truth.

> *"When he has brought out all his own, he goes on ahead of them, and his sheep follow him because they know his voice. But they will never follow a stranger; in fact, they will run away from him because they do not recognize a stranger's voice." (John 10:4–5 NIV)*

> *"My sheep listen to my voice; I know them, and they follow me." (John 10:27 NIV)*

Meditation is one of the primary ways believers learn to recognize the voice of the Shepherd. While prayer is the act of speaking to God, meditation is the practice of slowing down, reflecting, and allowing His Word to settle deeply within our hearts and minds.

Meditation means to ponder, reflect, rehearse, and deeply focus on God's Word in His presence. It involves giving careful attention to truth so that it moves beyond intellectual knowledge and becomes lived understanding.

In the Hebrew language, the word most often translated meditate is *hagah*, which means to murmur, utter, or contemplate. It literally describes speaking the Word softly to oneself—turning it over repeatedly in the heart and mind until it becomes revelation.

> *"But his delight is in the law of the Lord, and on his law he meditates day and night." (Psalm 1:2)*

> *"I will meditate on your precepts and consider your ways." (Psalm 119:15)*

Meditation redirects the focus of our minds toward the things of God. Rather than allowing our thoughts to be shaped by fear, anxiety, or worldly distractions, meditation intentionally fills the mind with truth.

> *"Since, then, you have been raised with Christ, set your hearts on things above, where Christ is... Set your minds on things above, not on earthly things." (Colossians 3:1–2 NIV)*

> *"Finally, brothers and sisters, whatever is true, whatever is noble, whatever is right, whatever is pure, whatever is lovely, whatever is admirable—if anything is excellent or praiseworthy—think about such things." (Philippians 4:8 NIV)*

Through meditation, believers begin to internalize God's Word. Truth is no longer something merely read or heard—it becomes something that shapes our thinking, influences our decisions, and transforms our hearts.

Meditation can be thought of as spiritual digestion. Just as the body receives nourishment from food through digestion, the soul receives nourishment as God's Word is slowly absorbed through reflection and contemplation. Meditation takes what we have read, heard, or experienced in Scripture and allows it to nourish our inner life until it becomes part of who we are.

As we meditate on Scripture, our thoughts gradually align with God's truth, strengthening faith and developing spiritual discernment. Over time this practice deepens intimacy with the Lord, helping us recognize His voice more clearly and walk more confidently in His direction.

Prayer and meditation together form the rhythm of continual communion with God. They become the believer's lifeline—the place of spiritual renewal, the source of discernment, and the pathway through which transformation takes place.

> *"Come near to God and he will come near to you."*
> *(James 4:8 NIV)*

Where reading the Word gives information, meditation produces transformation.

THE POWER AND PROMISE OF MEDITATION

God directly links spiritual success, stability, and victory to meditating on His Word. Scripture teaches that meditation anchors our lives in obedience and allows God's truth to shape our thoughts, actions, and direction.

> *"Keep this Book of the Law always on your lips; meditate on it day and night, so that you may be careful to do everything written in it. Then you will be prosperous and successful."*
> *(Joshua 1:8 NIV)*

When believers meditate on Scripture, the Holy Spirit inscribes truth upon the heart, shaping the inner life to reflect God's nature. Thoughts gradually begin to align with His truth, and old mental strongholds begin to lose their influence.

As God's truth takes root, the fruit of the Spirit becomes increasingly visible in attitudes, responses, and emotions. Meditation renews the inner life, transforming the heart and mind so that they increasingly reflect the character of Christ.

MEDITATION AND SPIRITUAL WARFARE

Meditation also plays a crucial role in spiritual warfare because the primary battlefield of spiritual conflict is the mind. The enemy often seeks to influence thoughts through fear, accusation, deception, and distorted beliefs. When the mind is filled with God's truth, those lies lose their power.

A mind anchored in the Word becomes strengthened against deception and guarded by the peace of God.

> *"We demolish arguments and every pretension that sets itself up against the knowledge of God, and we take captive every thought to make it obedient to Christ." (2 Corinthians 10:5)*

WHEN TO MEDITATE

Meditating day and night (Psalm 1:2) describes cultivating an ongoing awareness of God—an inward conversation with Him that continues throughout the rhythms of daily life.

> *"But whose delight is in the law of the Lord, and who meditates on his law day and night." (Psalm 1:2 NIV)*

> *"When I remember You on my bed, I meditate on You in the night watches." (Psalm 63:6 NIV)*

> *"My eyes stay open through the watches of the night, that I may meditate on Your promises." (Psalm 119:148 NIV)*

Meditation is not an escape from reality—it is an intimate encounter with God through His truth. Stillness before Him is not empty silence; it is sacred attentiveness, a quiet awareness that He is near. It is trusting that He hears when we speak, attuning our hearts to listen for His voice, and resting as He works within and through our lives.

Through this practice the soul is healed, the spirit strengthened, and the heart gradually transformed.

"Be still, and know that I am God." (Psalm 46:10 NIV)

The goal of prayer and meditation is not merely spiritual discipline—it is relationship with the God of the universe who already knows our name but invites us to know His heart. Over time, consistent communion with God deepens our awareness of His presence and strengthens our connection with Him.

As we learn to speak with Him in prayer and listen through meditation on His Word, our hearts begin to align with His truth, His character, and His purposes. Long-term communion with God reshapes the way we think, respond, and live. Fear gradually gives way to trust, decisions become guided by wisdom rather than impulse, and our lives increasingly reflect the character of Christ.

Through this ongoing relationship, God not only heals and strengthens us—He prepares us. As believers learn to hear His voice and walk in His truth, they grow in discernment, compassion, and faithfulness.

In this way, prayer and meditation connect personal transformation with eternal purpose. They deepen our relationship with God and prepare us to live faithfully in the work He has entrusted to His people.

LIVING IN CONTINUAL COMMUNION

Prayer and meditation invite believers into a life of continual communion with God. These practices are not merely spiritual disciplines to perform but pathways into relationship with the One who created us and redeemed us.

Through prayer we bring our hearts before the Lord—our gratitude, our struggles, our needs, and our praise. Through meditation we slow down long enough to reflect upon His Word and allow His truth to shape our thoughts and guide our lives. Together they form a rhythm of communication with God that strengthens faith and deepens spiritual awareness.

Over time this ongoing communion begins to reshape the inner life. Fear gives way to trust, confusion yields to wisdom, and the voice of the Shepherd becomes easier to recognize. As believers remain anchored in God's presence, their hearts grow more sensitive to His leading and their lives increasingly reflect the character of Christ.

In this way, prayer and meditation do more than sustain personal faith—they cultivate the spiritual awareness necessary to walk faithfully with God in every area of life. They keep the believer rooted in truth, attentive to the Holy Spirit, and prepared for whatever work God places before them.

As believers grow in this rhythm of prayer and meditation, their relationship with God deepens and their spiritual awareness becomes clearer. Time spent in His presence not only strengthens personal faith, but also prepares the heart for the work He desires to accomplish through His people.

Throughout Scripture we see that God often prepares His servants in the quiet places of communion before sending them into the world. Moses encountered God in the wilderness before leading Israel. David learned to worship the Lord in the fields before ruling as king. Jesus Himself withdrew regularly to pray before carrying out His ministry among the people.

In the same way, believers today are shaped and prepared through time spent with the Lord. Prayer aligns the heart with His will, and meditation anchors the mind in His truth. As we learn to listen for His voice and walk in step with His Spirit, we begin to recognize where He is leading and how He desires to work through our lives.

This ongoing communion with God strengthens discernment, deepens trust, and cultivates humility—qualities that are essential for anyone who seeks to serve in the work of the Kingdom. The more closely we walk with Him, the more clearly we begin to understand His heart for others and His desire to bring healing, restoration, and freedom to a broken world.

Over time, the freedom we have received becomes something we carry. The truth that has renewed our minds becomes truth we share. The grace we have experienced becomes grace we extend to others.

In this way, communion with God does more than sustain our own freedom—it prepares us to participate in the work of His Kingdom.

In the next chapter we will explore what it means to step into that calling. Scripture teaches that those who follow Christ are not only recipients of His grace but also participants in His mission. As believers grow in maturity and surrender, they are invited to take part in the ministry of reconciliation—extending the freedom they have received to others.

Reflection Questions

1. Take a few moments to reflect honestly on your relationship with God through prayer and meditation.
2. Do I approach prayer as a conversation with God or primarily as a list of requests?
3. How regularly do I take time to meditate on Scripture and allow it to shape my thinking?
4. Am I learning to recognize the voice of the Shepherd in my life?
5. In what ways might God be inviting me to deepen my time with Him?

Allow these questions to guide a quiet moment of reflection before the Lord.

Prayer

Lord,

Thank You for inviting me into relationship with You. Teach me to come before You with honesty, humility, and faith. Help me grow in prayer so that my heart becomes more attentive to Your presence and Your voice.

As I meditate on Your Word, renew my mind and align my thoughts with Your truth. Guard my heart from deception, strengthen my faith, and help me walk in the freedom You have given.

Draw me closer to You each day and shape my life so that it reflects Your character and Your love. In Jesus' name, Amen.

Chapter 11
BATTLE READY & EQUIPPED

*"Very truly I tell you, whoever believes in me will do the
works I have been doing, and they will do
even greater things than these, because I am
going to the Father"— John 14:12 NIV*

Throughout this book we have explored how Christ brings freedom into the life of the believer—breaking the power of sin, healing wounded places of the heart, and restoring what the enemy has sought to destroy. Yet the work of freedom does not end with personal restoration. God often uses those who have experienced His freedom to help others find it as well.

As believers grow in freedom and understanding, they begin to recognize that salvation is not only about what we are saved from—it is also about what we are saved for. We are not merely delivered from sin and death but redeemed for His divine purpose. The freedom Christ gives is never meant to remain contained within our own lives. It becomes something we carry—something that begins to overflow into the lives of others.

From the beginning of His ministry, Jesus called ordinary people to follow Him, learn from Him, and eventually participate in the work of His Kingdom. Those who walked with Him were not only taught—they were prepared, shaped, and ultimately sent.

Before ascending into heaven, Jesus entrusted this calling to His followers when He gave what has come to be known as the

Great Commission:

> *"Therefore go and make disciples of all nations." (Matthew 28:19–20, NIV).*

Jesus calls His followers saints, ministers, and ambassadors for a reason. He appoints, anoints, and sends them on missions ordained by His hand.

> *"We are therefore Christ's ambassadors, as though God were making his appeal through us." (2 Corinthians 5:20, NIV).*

Just as an ambassador is never sent without provision, God supplies everything necessary to fulfill the assignment He gives. In Christ, with the Holy Spirit dwelling within us, we are equipped and prepared. His calling is always accompanied by His anointing, His equipping, and His Spirit.

For this reason, believers who desire to serve others must remain rooted in Christ. In the previous chapter we explored the practices of prayer and meditation—learning to quiet our hearts, listen for the voice of God, and anchor our lives in His truth. These practices are not separate from the work of the Kingdom; they are the foundation of it.

It is in prayer that our hearts are aligned with God's will, our minds are renewed by His truth, and our spirits are strengthened through communion with Him.

SALVATION MUST COME FIRST

As believers participate in the work of the Kingdom, it is important to keep the heart of the mission clear. While the fullness of freedom, healing, and restoration is a beautiful expression of God's Kingdom—and undeniably a worthy pursuit—salvation must always remain the starting point.

The message of reconciliation with God is the foundation

upon which all other transformation rests. Without salvation, the deeper work of healing and restoration cannot fully take root in the way God intends.

Complete healing in every dimension of life may not be fully realized on this side of eternity. Much of the restoration God accomplishes unfolds gradually as we continue walking with Christ. Yet the gift of salvation stands as the essential beginning. It is certain, foundational, and eternal. It opens the door to transformation and is the priceless gift of God, purchased at the highest cost—the very life of Jesus Christ.

Through salvation we are not only restored to relationship with God—we are also invited into His purposes. Those who are made new in Christ are called to participate in the work of His Kingdom, extending His grace and truth to others.

Scripture reminds us:

"For it is by grace you have been saved, through faith… it is the gift of God." (Ephesians 2:8–9, NIV)

And further:

"We are God's handiwork, created in Christ Jesus to do good works, which God prepared in advance for us to do." (Ephesians 2:10, NIV).

In this way, salvation becomes both the beginning of transformation and the doorway into the life of purpose God has prepared for His people.

EQUIPPED BY THE SPIRIT AND EACH OTHER

When God calls His people into the work of His Kingdom, He does not leave them to carry out that calling in their own strength. The same Lord who commissions His followers also equips them for the work He has entrusted to them.

Throughout Scripture we see that God prepares those He sends. He provides wisdom, guidance, spiritual authority, and the presence of the Holy Spirit to lead and strengthen His people. What God calls a person to accomplish, He also supplies the resources necessary to fulfill.

God never intended His people to rely solely on their own ability. Instead, He invites them to depend on His truth, His Spirit, and the wisdom He provides through His Word and through the Body of Christ.

As believers learn to rely on these provisions rather than their own strength, they become better prepared to serve others with humility, discernment, and faithfulness. One important safeguard God provides in this process is the ongoing practice of seeking wise counsel from trusted Christian brethren, coupled with complete dependence on the leading and power of the Holy Spirit.

Scripture highlights the value of a multitude of counsel as a divine safeguard. It tempers pride, sharpens discernment, exposes blind spots, and confirms direction. As it is written, "For lack of guidance a nation falls, but victory is won through many advisers" (Proverbs 11:14).

Leaders who pursue wise counsel do not weaken their authority—they strengthen and protect it. Once insight has been received from spiritually mature voices, that collective wisdom must then be brought before the Lord in prayer. His confirmation is essential and should be sought before responding to any matter at hand. Ultimately, Jesus Himself is the Wonderful Counselor (Isaiah 9:6).

The value of a multitude of counsel also depends greatly on the character of those providing it. If you surround yourself with people-pleasers—"yes men" or "yes women"—you may hear what you want to hear rather than what you truly need to hear. Scripture warns that in the last days people will gather teachers to say what their "itching ears want to hear" (2 Timothy 4:3).

A healthy counselor, pastor, or trusted friend must be willing to speak truth with courage and love, even at the risk of discomfort or relational strain. "Wounds from a friend can be trusted" (Proverbs 27:6). A true friend lovingly offers honest counsel, not flattery, valuing your safety and growth more than their own personal comfort. They are willing to risk tension in the relationship in order to speak truth with integrity.

In some situations, we may be the ones called to provide wise counsel to others. At other times, we must be humble enough to surround ourselves with people who can offer that same counsel to us. This mutual exchange of wisdom is one of the ways the Body of Christ functions as God intended. As believers walk together in humility and dependence upon the Lord, we become instruments through which His wisdom is shared—serving as the eyes and ears of Christ for one another as He leads, corrects, and guides His people.

In addition to the wisdom God provides through the community of believers, He also equips His people through the spiritual gifts given by the Holy Spirit.

EXERCISING THE GIFTS

All followers of Christ carry the gifts of the Spirit within them through the indwelling presence of the Holy Spirit. While certain gifts may appear more prominent in a person's life—what we might call dominant gifts—others may operate more quietly in the background. Yet all are available according to the Spirit's leading. Some gifts are exercised regularly as part of a believer's daily walk and service, while others may emerge in specific moments when they are needed.

It is wise to pursue and develop the gifts we carry so we can learn how to faithfully and uniquely share what God has entrusted to us. As we grow in understanding how the Holy Spirit works through us, we become better stewards of the grace placed within our lives. These gifts are not given for personal recognition, but so that the life and love of Christ can be extended to others through us.

The Holy Spirit is the One who sends, equips, and releases the gifts needed to accomplish God's purposes. As believers walk in surrender to Him, He supplies what is required in each moment—wisdom when guidance is needed, discernment when clarity is required, encouragement when hearts need strengthening, and healing or deliverance when freedom is being restored.

THE BELIEVER'S MARCHING ORDERS

The Great Commission is, quite literally, the believer's marching orders—spoken directly from the mouth of our Lord. Jesus did not simply give instructions; He first modeled the way. Throughout His ministry He demonstrated how the Kingdom of God operates—proclaiming truth, healing the sick, restoring the broken, and setting captives free.

After teaching and equipping His followers, He sent them out as extensions of His own ministry, carrying forward the work He began.

The very Spirit who dwelt in Jesus—the same Spirit who raised Him from the dead—now lives within every person who chooses to follow Him. Because of this, the mission of Christ did not end with His earthly ministry; it continues through the lives of His people. What He demonstrated, He now empowers His followers to carry forward.

Just before ascending into heaven, Jesus entrusted this mission to all who would believe, passing the baton of Kingdom purpose into the hands of His followers. He said:

"All authority in heaven and on earth has been given to me. Therefore go and make disciples of all nations, baptizing them and teaching them to obey everything I have commanded you. And surely I am with you always, to the very end of the age." (Matthew 28:18–20)

Jesus, possessing all authority, sends out His people in His power to every nation—to proclaim the gospel, make disciples, baptize them, and teach them to obey His commands. The message of salvation was not meant to remain information alone; it was meant to lead people into transformation and a new way of life under the lordship of Christ.

Through discipleship, believers are guided into maturity, learning to walk in truth, live by the Spirit, and reflect the character of Jesus in their daily lives. And with this commission comes His unfailing promise: He will be with us every step of the way.

He also called His followers to be living examples of what He had taught. Their lives were to reflect His character, demonstrating the love, humility, compassion, and authority of the Kingdom. The attributes of Christ—now dwelling within them through the Holy Spirit—become visible to the world as they exercise the gifts and authority He has entrusted to them.

The mission itself was clear and practical:

• Heal the sick
• Cast out demons
• Set captives free
• Proclaim the good news

This calling is not sustained by human effort, religious systems, or personal striving. The work of the Kingdom flows from what Jesus described as new wine—the life of the Spirit—poured into new wineskins. Spirit-filled believers become those new wineskins—people whose lives have been renewed and who are willing to carry the life of the Spirit wherever they go.

As they remain surrendered to God, the Holy Spirit moves through them, releasing the power and grace of the New Covenant into the lives of others.

Because of this, the believer's role is not to manufacture results but to remain connected to the Source. As we walk in surrender and obedience, the Spirit supplies what is needed for ministry and service.

And in this calling, we are never left to rely on our own strength. God Himself guarantees the provision and equipping necessary for the work He assigns:

> *"His divine power has given us everything we need for a godly life." (2 Peter 1:3, NIV)*

MANNING YOUR POST

The One who calls will use those He has called according to His wisdom and purposes. Each person's assignment unfolds in the way God intends, and in His timing. Yet before someone can effectively help others experience freedom, they must first encounter that freedom themselves. Genuine growth and personal transformation become the foundation from which we are able to serve others with integrity and understanding.

When the Lord calls a person into a particular area of ministry, He does not leave them to figure it out on their own. He prepares, anoints, and equips those He sends. God often works through ordinary people, using His followers as vessels through which He carries out His work. The power and effectiveness of ministry do not come from human ability alone, but from the Spirit of God working through surrendered lives.

Because of this, the servant's responsibility is twofold: to pursue and safeguard their own freedom while helping others discover theirs. As we continue walking with Christ, we remain attentive to our own growth, allowing Him to heal, refine, and strengthen us along the way.

This transformation happens through time spent with Jesus—our Teacher, Director, Guide, and Protector. As we remain in His presence, He shapes our character and renews our hearts.

Ultimately, every believer faces a choice in how they approach the work of the Kingdom. We can attempt to do His work for Him through our own effort and striving, relying on personal strength and ability. Or we can surrender ourselves fully to Him and allow Him to accomplish His work through us. Only the latter produces lasting fruit, because it flows not from human effort but from the life and power of God working within us.

EFFECTIVELY PURSUING HIS OBJECTIVE

As followers of Christ, we are not called merely to speak about the Kingdom—we are commissioned to live within it and actively participate in its work. The life of the believer is not simply a belief system or a set of teachings to agree with; it is a calling to embody the message of the gospel in both word and action.

Jesus made it clear that His mission had now become the mission of His followers. In describing His own purpose, He declared:

"He has sent me to proclaim freedom for the prisoners and recovery of sight for the blind, to set the oppressed free…"(Luke 4:18–19 NIV)

This mission did not end with His earthly ministry. Jesus entrusted the same work to those who follow Him. As believers walk in faith and surrender, signs of the Kingdom accompany their lives:

"In my name they will drive out demons… they will place their hands on sick people, and they will get well." (Mark 16:17–18 NIV)

When Jesus first sent His disciples out, He gave them clear instructions about both the message and the ministry of the Kingdom:

"As you go, proclaim this message: 'The kingdom of heaven has come near.' Heal the sick, raise the dead, cleanse those who have leprosy, drive out demons. Freely you have re-

ceived; freely give." (Matthew 10:7–8 NIV)

Freely we have received His Spirit, forgiveness, grace, mercy, healing, and deliverance—and freely we are now called to share it with the world. Having been entrusted with such gifts, we become His hands, His feet, and His voice to a hurting, bound, and broken world, extending to others what He has so generously bestowed upon us.

> *"From everyone who has been given much, much will be demanded; and from the one who has been entrusted with much, much more will be asked." (Luke 12:48 NIV)*

To walk and live in the Spirit, rather than in the flesh, means surrendering self and allowing the Holy Spirit to govern our thoughts, desires, decisions, and actions instead of being driven by our emotions and fallen nature. The flesh represents self-centered impulses, worldly cravings, pride, fear, and reactions rooted in the old life.

True servanthood is not about achieving perfection but rather choosing His direction. It is a daily conscious decision to yield to the Spirit's leading, to crucify selfish impulses, and to cultivate the fruit of righteousness. This applies to every believer.

> *"Very truly I tell you, whoever believes in me will do the works I have been doing, and they will do even greater things than these, because I am going to the Father." (John 14:12 NIV)*

Jesus' own mission statement:

> *"He has sent me to proclaim freedom for the prisoners and recovery of sight for the blind, to set the oppressed free..." (Luke 4:18–19 NIV)*

Signs that follow those who believe:

> *"In my name they will drive out demons… they will place their hands on sick people, and they will get well." (Mark 16:17–18 NIV)*

When Jesus sent the disciples out:

> *"As you go, proclaim this message: 'The kingdom of heaven has come near.' Heal the sick, raise the dead, cleanse those who have leprosy, drive out demons. Freely you have received; freely give." (Matthew 10:7–8 NIV)*

When serving as ambassadors for Christ, it is wise to pause and ask ourselves some key questions.

The work of the Kingdom is carried not by striving, but by surrender—by new wine flowing through new wineskins, hearts made new and continually filled with the Holy Spirit. He assures us that we will not be left lacking:

> *"His divine power has given us everything we need" (2 Peter 1:3, NIV).*

SELF-REFLECTION FOR READINESS TO SERVE

Readiness to serve flows from a place of inner freedom and connection with Jesus. It is not about meeting a rigid checklist or proving ourselves worthy. Instead, it grows out of identity, empowerment, and the gentle work of the Holy Spirit within us.

Each of us can only offer what we are currently living from. As we continue to grow in freedom, love, and truth, that is what naturally overflows to others. When areas of our own heart still need healing, it doesn't disqualify us—it simply invites us to come closer to Jesus, to receive more of His grace, and to continue our own journey of transformation.

These reflections are not meant to bring pressure or shame. They are simply a way to notice where your heart is and to invite Jesus into those places. Let them become a conversation between you and Him.

Take a moment to sit with the Lord and consider each question with honesty and kindness toward yourself:

What is motivating my heart right now?
Am I seeking recognition, or am I seeking to glorify Christ?

> *"Am I now trying to win the approval of human beings, or of God?" (Galatians 1:10)*

Where is my love flowing from?
Am I serving out of love for Him and others, or from a sense of pressure or obligation?

> *"If I do not have love, I gain nothing." (1 Corinthians 13:3)*

What posture is my heart taking?
Is there humility and openness, or do I notice places of striving or self-focus?

> *"In humility value others above yourselves." (Philippians 2:3)*

Where am I drawing my strength from?
Am I relying on my own effort, or leaning on the Holy Spirit's power?

> *Not by might nor by power, but by my Spirit." (Zechariah 4:6)*

Am I making space to listen to Him?
Am I pausing to hear His voice before I act?
> *"My sheep listen to my voice… and they follow me."*
> *(John 10:27)*

How do I respond to timing?
Do I trust His timing, or do I feel the need to rush ahead?

> *"He has made everything beautiful in its time." (Ecclesiastes 3:11)*

What is my focus in serving?
Am I building up the Body of Christ, or trying to prove something about myself?

> *"To equip his people for works of service, so that the body of Christ may be built up." (Ephesians 4:12)*

How am I treating others along the way?
Do my words and actions reflect the compassion, patience, and kindness of Jesus?

> *"Therefore, as God's chosen people, holy and dearly loved, clothe yourselves with compassion, kindness, humility, gentleness and patience."(Colossians 3:12 NIV)*

A FINAL INVITATION

Wherever you see growth, give thanks. Wherever you recognize areas still in process, receive grace.

This journey has never been about achieving perfection. It has always been about returning to truth, embracing healing, and living in the abiding presence of Jesus within you. He is not asking you to strive harder; He is inviting you to live more deeply connected, more fully surrendered, and more securely rooted in His love.

As you continue forward, you will discover that freedom is not merely something you receive—it becomes something you carry. The healing you have embraced begins to overflow. The truth that has renewed your mind becomes light for others. The grace you have received becomes the grace you extend. The freedom within you becomes freedom flowing through you.

This is how the Kingdom of God moves through the world—one life transformed, one heart restored, one person walking in truth and freedom at a time.

The journey you have walked in this chapter is not the end of the story. It is preparation. As God continues to deepen your understanding and strengthen your walk with Him, He may also open doors for you to help others experience the same freedom you have received.

In the next chapter, we will begin exploring how believers can participate in the ministry of healing and deliverance—learning how to recognize spiritual bondage, how freedom is restored through Christ, and how to walk in this work with humility, discernment, and dependence on the Holy Spirit.

For those who are willing to remain close to Him, the freedom God has placed within you may become the very freedom He uses to set others free.

Prayer
Lord Jesus,
Thank You for the work You have begun in my life. Thank You for the truth that sets me free and for the grace that meets me in every place where I am still growing. I surrender my heart to You again today. Continue to heal what is wounded, renew what has been distorted, and strengthen what You are building within me. Teach me to walk in Your Spirit rather than in my own strength. Help me to trust Your timing, follow Your voice, and remain rooted in Your love. Use my life as a vessel of Your grace. Let

the freedom I have received become freedom that flows through to others. Where there is pain, let me carry Your compassion. Where there is confusion, let me carry Your truth. Where there is bondage, let me carry the hope of Your restoration.

Above all Lord, keep my heart close to You. Let my life reflect Your goodness, Your mercy, and Your power.

I offer myself to You—my past, my present, and my future. Lead me wherever You desire, and let my life be a testimony of Your redeeming love. In Jesus' name, - Amen.

Chapter 12
A CALLING TO DELIVERANCE & HEALING MINISTRY

"The Spirit of the Lord is on me, because he has anointed me to proclaim good news to the poor. He has sent me to proclaim freedom for the prisoners - and recovery of sight for the blind, to set the oppressed" —Luke 4:18 NIV

In the previous chapter, we explored the calling placed upon every believer to participate in the work of God's Kingdom. Salvation not only restores us to relationship with God—it also invites us to take part in His mission. Those who have received freedom are often called to help others experience that same freedom.

For many believers, this calling develops into a deeper desire to serve others through ministries of healing, restoration, and deliverance. Some will step into prayer ministries within the church. Others may be called to counseling, coaching, pastoral care, or specialized healing and deliverance ministries that help individuals overcome spiritual, emotional, and relational bondage.

Whatever the form of service may be, the heart of this calling remains the same: God often uses those who have personally encountered His healing to help guide others toward freedom.

Jesus expressed this principle clearly when He instructed His disciples:

"Freely you have received; freely give."(Matthew 10:8)

Those who have experienced the restoring work of Christ often carry a deeper compassion for those who are still struggling. Their testimony becomes living evidence that God continues to heal, restore, and set captives free.

At the same time, stepping into a ministry that helps others find freedom carries great responsibility. Healing and deliverance ministry should never be approached casually or as a demonstration of spiritual ability. True ministry flows from humility, spiritual maturity, and a deep dependence upon the Holy Spirit.

Believers who feel called into this work must recognize that they are not the source of freedom—Jesus is. Those who minister simply serve as vessels through which Jesus extends His authority, compassion, and truth.

At the same time, freedom requires a willing heart. While God provides the authority and power to bring deliverance, the person receiving ministry must also choose to turn toward truth and walk away from the patterns or agreements that once held them in bondage.

Scripture reminds us of this responsibility:

> *"I have set before you life and death, blessings and curses. Now choose life, so that you and your children may live."* *(Deuteronomy 30:19)*

Deliverance ministry therefore involves both the power of God and the cooperation of the individual. God provides the authority, truth, and power to set people free, while the person receiving ministry must be willing to walk in the freedom that Christ offers.

As we begin exploring the ministry of healing and deliverance more directly, it is important to remember that this work is not carried out through personal strength or spiritual ambition. It flows from faith, humility, and dependence upon the Holy Spirit.

FAITH IS A NECESSITY

Faith plays a central role in the ministry of healing and deliverance. Everyone involved must believe that Jesus still heals the brokenhearted, restores the wounded, and sets captives free.

Faith is the foundation upon which believers approach God, trust His character, and receive His work. Without faith, it becomes difficult to recognize or receive what God desires to do.

Scripture explains this clearly:

"Now faith is the substance of things hoped for, the evidence of things not seen." (Hebrews 11:1)

Faith allows believers to trust that Christ's authority is real and active even when the outcome has not yet been seen. It anchors the heart in God's promises and reminds us that freedom ultimately flows from the finished work of Jesus.

"And without faith it is impossible to please God, because anyone who comes to him must believe that he exists and that he rewards those who earnestly seek him."(Hebrews 11:6)

For those serving in healing and deliverance ministry, faith becomes the posture through which the work is approached. It keeps the focus on Christ rather than on human ability and reminds us that true freedom is always the result of God's power at work.

At the same time, those who minister to others must approach this work with humility, discernment, and dependence upon the Holy Spirit. The goal is never to demonstrate spiritual authority or personal power, but to help restore individuals to the freedom and wholeness God intends.

THE GREAT PHYSICIAN'S PRESCRIPTION

As you step into the ministry of healing and deliverance, it is essential to remember that the source of all healing is not human effort, spiritual ability, or personal authority. Jesus Himself—*Jehovah Rapha,* the God who heals, the Great Physician—is the One who restores what has been broken.

Just as a physician provides a prescription to guide the healing of the body, Christ has provided His Word to guide and equip you in the work of spiritual restoration. Scripture forms the foundation for understanding the nature of spiritual bondage, the authority of Christ, and the path that leads people toward healing and freedom.

Through God's Word you receive instruction, correction, wisdom, and training for the work He calls you to do. As Paul reminds us:

> *"All Scripture is God-breathed and is useful for teaching, rebuking, correcting and training in righteousness, so that the servant of God may be thoroughly equipped for every good work." (2 Timothy 3:16–17)*

When you minister to someone seeking freedom, God's Word provides the truth needed to address spiritual, emotional, and relational struggles. It gives you the wisdom to recognize deception, expose the enemy's influence, and guide the individual back into alignment with God's truth.

Yet Scripture alone is not meant to function apart from the work of the Holy Spirit. As you minister, the Holy Spirit illuminates the Word, bringing clarity to what is taking place beneath the surface. He reveals hidden wounds, exposes lies that have been believed, and brings conviction where repentance and healing are needed. In this way, the Spirit of God applies the Word of God to the heart of the person receiving ministry.

The psalmist describes the power of God's Word in this way:

"He sent out His word and healed them; He rescued them from the grave." (Psalm 107:20)

As someone serving in healing and deliverance ministry, you must learn to rely on both the truth of Scripture and the leading of the Holy Spirit. The Word reveals what is true, while the Spirit brings that truth into the specific circumstances of the individual—exposing deception, dismantling lies, and guiding them toward freedom.

When these two work together—God's Word and God's Spirit—areas that have been shaped by sin, deception, wounds, or spiritual influence begin to come into the light. Truth replaces lies, healing begins to restore what has been broken, and the authority of Christ reclaims what once stood in bondage.

For this reason, remain firmly grounded in Scripture while staying attentive to the voice of the Holy Spirit. Your role is not simply to confront spiritual darkness, but to help guide people into the truth that sets them free.

As Jesus Himself declared:

"If you hold to my teaching, you are really my disciples. Then you will know the truth, and the truth will set you free." (John 8:31–32)

UNDERSTANDING HOW BONDAGE DEVELOPS

Because healing and deliverance ministry seeks to guide people into freedom, it is also important to understand how bondage develops in the first place. Without recognizing the roots of spiritual and emotional strongholds, it is easy to focus only on outward symptoms while the deeper causes remain unaddressed.

For this reason, those who minister to others must develop an understanding of how wounds, deception, and spiritual influence can gradually shape a person's life.

Spiritual bondage doesn't develops in isolation. In most cases, it forms gradually through a combination of wounds, deception, sin, and spiritual influence.

People often come for ministry because they are experiencing anxiety, fear, depression, destructive patterns, or spiritual oppression. While these struggles may appear on the surface as emotional or behavioral problems, deeper roots are often involved.

In many situations, wounds from past experiences create openings where lies begin to take root. A person who has experienced rejection may begin to believe they are unlovable. Someone who has endured abuse may come to believe they are powerless or worthless. Over time, these beliefs can shape a person's identity and influence the choices they make.

Jesus spoke about the destructive power of deception when He described the work of the enemy:

> *"The thief comes only to steal and kill and destroy; I have come that they may have life, and have it to the full."* (John 10:10)

The enemy often works by reinforcing lies that have already taken root in a wounded heart. When those lies are believed, they begin to shape behavior, emotions, and spiritual outlook.

At times, persistent sin or unhealthy coping patterns can also deepen these areas of bondage. Habits formed in response to pain may initially feel like protection, but over time they can create patterns that keep a person trapped in cycles they feel unable to break.

In some cases, spiritual oppression may also be involved. Demonic influence does not always appear in dramatic ways. More often it operates subtly, reinforcing lies, increasing confusion, and amplifying the wounds a person already carries.

For this reason, healing and deliverance ministry must address both the spiritual and personal dimensions of a person's struggle. True freedom often requires bringing wounds into the light, confronting deception with truth, and inviting the authority of Jesus Christ to break the influence of anything that has kept the person in bondage.

As you minister to others, remember that your role is not to force change but to help reveal the truth. The Holy Spirit exposes what has been hidden and gently leads individuals toward repentance, healing, and restoration.

When lies are replaced with truth and wounds are brought before the healing presence of Christ, the power of bondage begins to weaken and the path toward freedom becomes clear.

Common Doors That Allow Bondage

As these root issues begin to emerge, certain patterns often become visible. Scripture and ministry experience both reveal that bondage frequently enters through identifiable doors—places where wounds, deception, or sin have created openings for spiritual oppression.

Understanding these patterns does not mean approaching ministry with suspicion or fear. Instead, it provides clarity and helps guide prayer, discernment, and the process of healing. This includes:

Unresolved Wounds

One of the most common doors is unresolved wounds and trauma. Experiences such as rejection, abandonment, abuse, or betrayal can leave deep emotional injuries. When these wounds remain unhealed, they can shape the way a person sees themselves, others, and even God.

Unforgiveness and Bitterness

Another common door is unforgiveness. When individuals carry bitterness or resentment, it can create spiritual and emotional bondage. Jesus spoke directly about the importance of forgiveness, reminding His followers that withholding forgiveness can affect a person's spiritual freedom.

"Forgive, and you will be forgiven." (Luke 6:37)

Agreements with Lies

Agreements with lies can also play a powerful role in maintaining bondage. When a person repeatedly believes false messages such as "I am worthless," "God has abandoned me," or "I will never change," those beliefs begin to shape their reality.

Addictions

In some cases, habitual sin, counterfeit comforts or destructive patterns may also contribute to bondage. These patterns often require awareness, repentance and intentional change as individuals learn to walk in new ways of living.

Occult Practices

There are also situations where involvement with occult practices or spiritual counterfeits can open doors to spiritual oppression. Activities that seek supernatural guidance or power outside of God can invite spiritual influences that oppose the work of Christ.

Generational Patterns

Generational patterns may sometimes appear in a person's life. Families can pass down patterns of behavior, belief, or spiritual influence that affect future generations.

As you minister healing and deliverance, these doors are not meant to bring condemnation. Rather, they help identify areas where God's truth and healing are needed.

The goal of ministry is not to expose someone's past in order to bring shame, but to bring hidden things into the light so that Christ can restore what has been broken.

UNDERSTANDING SPIRITUAL FOOTHOLDS

Scripture also refers to these areas as spiritual footholds that develop in their lives. A foothold can be understood as a place of influence—an area where deception, wounds, or sinful patterns have created an opening for the enemy to gain access.

The apostle Paul cautioned believers about this when he wrote:

"Do not give the devil a foothold." (Ephesians 4:27)

Footholds often develop when wounds remain unresolved, lies are believed as truth, or sinful patterns are allowed to continue without repentance.

Over time, these areas can become deeply embedded in a person's thinking and behavior, forming the strongholds that keep individuals trapped in cycles of bondage.

Understanding spiritual footholds helps ministers approach healing and deliverance with greater wisdom. Rather than reacting only to surface symptoms, it allows them to recognize the deeper areas that must be addressed for lasting freedom to occur.

As these footholds are exposed through truth, repentance, forgiveness, and prayer, the influence they once held begins to weaken.

When individuals bring these areas into the light and surrender them to Christ, the authority of Jesus replaces the influence that once kept them bound. Out of the arms of the false comforter and into the arms of Jesus, the True Comforter.

DISCERNING THE NATURE OF THE STRUGGLE

As you begin ministering to others, one of the most important spiritual gifts you can develop is spiritual discernment. Not every struggle a person experiences has the same source, and effective ministry requires wisdom to recognize what is truly taking place.

Some struggles are rooted in emotional wounds, trauma, or broken relationships. Others may involve deeply ingrained patterns of sin, destructive beliefs, or spiritual deception. In certain cases, spiritual oppression or demonic influence may also be present.

Because these issues can often overlap, it is important to approach each situation with humility and patience rather than rushing to conclusions. Deliverance ministry is not about quickly labeling problems or assuming a spiritual cause for every difficulty because most struggles are multi-faceted. Instead, it involves listening carefully, observing thoughtfully, and seeking the guidance of the Holy Spirit.

Scripture reminds us that discernment is a gift given by the Spirit:

"To another is given… distinguishing between spirits."(1 Corinthians 12:10)

As you minister, the Holy Spirit helps you recognize what lies be- neath the surface of a person's struggle. He may bring insight through prayer, through the person's story, or through patterns that begin to emerge as you listen.

Often, the key to understanding what someone is facing is found in the areas where pain, deception, and spiritual influence intersect. Wounds may create vulnerabilities. Lies may shape beliefs about God, self, or others. And in some cases, spiritual forces may seek to reinforce those lies in order to keep a person bound.

For this reason, effective healing and deliverance ministry requires both spiritual sensitivity and careful listening. Your role is not to force answers or attempt to control the process, but to partner with the Holy Spirit as He reveals what needs to be addressed.

As truth begins to surface, the path toward healing and freedom becomes clearer. The Holy Spirit brings what has been hidden into the light so that the authority of Christ can restore what has been broken.

In every situation, remember that Jesus is the true Deliverer. You are simply participating in the work He is already doing in the life of the person He places before you.

PREPARING THE PERSON FOR FREEDOM

Once these doors and root causes have been identified, the focus naturally shifts toward preparing the individual to receive healing and freedom. Lasting deliverance requires a willingness to bring hidden areas into the light and respond to God's truth.

As someone ministering in this area, your role is not to rush the process but to help guide the person toward readiness. The Holy Spirit works gently and intentionally, bringing areas into the light so that they can be addressed in proper order. These steps include:

Identifying wounds, sinful patterns and unhealthy coping mechanisms:

One of the most important steps in preparation is helping the per- son recognize and acknowledge areas where change is needed. This may involve identifying wounds, sinful patterns, unhealthy coping mechanisms, or agreements with lies that have shaped their thinking.

Repentance (walking towards God instead of away from Him)

Repentance is often part of this process. Repentance is not simply feeling remorse for past actions; it involves a willingness to turn away from what has been destructive and move toward the truth and life God offers.

Forgiveness

Forgiveness is another critical step in preparing the heart for freedom. Many people carry deep pain caused by the actions of others, and that pain can keep them bound emotionally and spiritually. As you minister, you may need to gently guide individuals toward releasing forgiveness—choosing to forgive the person who hurt them, not excusing or minimizing the wrongdoing, but releasing the hold that bitterness has on their own hearts. Forgiveness is not about justifying the offense; it is about freeing oneself from the burden of carrying it.

Jesus emphasized the importance of forgiveness when He taught His disciples to pray:

> *"Forgive us our debts, as we also have forgiven our debtors."*
> *(Matthew 6:12)*

Renounce Agreements

In addition to repentance and forgiveness, individuals may also need to renounce agreements with lies they have believed. Lies about their identity, their worth, or God's character can become deeply root- ed. As these lies are brought into the light, they can be replaced with the truth of Scripture.

Throughout this process, your role is to remain attentive to the Holy Spirit. He is the One who reveals what needs attention and who prepares the heart to receive freedom. Your responsibility is simply to guide the conversation, pray with discernment, and help the person respond to what God is revealing.

When a person becomes willing to bring hidden things into the light, extend forgiveness, and turn toward truth, the ground becomes prepared for the work of healing and deliverance to take place.

MINISTERING PRAYER FOR FREEDOM

Once a person has had the opportunity to prepare their heart through confession, repentance, forgiveness, and a willingness to embrace truth, the ministry of prayer for healing and deliverance can begin. As you enter this moment, it is important to remain calm, attentive, and fully dependent on the Holy Spirit.

Remember that you are not the source of freedom—Jesus is. Your role is simply to serve as a vessel through which Christ exercises His authority and extends His compassion to the individual seeking help.

Jesus demonstrated that authority when He ministered to those who were bound or oppressed. Through His word, He brought healing, restoration, and freedom to those who came to Him in faith. That same authority continues through His name today.

As Scripture declares:

"And these signs will accompany those who believe: In my name they will drive out demons..."(Mark 16:17)

When you minister deliverance, your authority rests entirely in the name of Jesus Christ and in the finished work of the cross. You do not need to raise your voice, perform dramatic actions, or attempt to force anything to happen. Instead, remain steady, prayerful, and attentive to the guidance of the Holy Spirit.

How to Start

Begin by inviting the presence of the Holy Spirit into the moment. Ask Him to reveal what needs to be addressed and to guide the process according to His wisdom. As you pray, you may sense areas that need to be brought into the light—wounds that need healing, lies that must be replaced with truth, or spiritual influences that must be confronted.

Deal with Demonic Activity

If demonic oppression is present, you may need to speak directly and firmly in the authority of Jesus Christ, commanding any unclean spirit to leave. This is not done with anger or fear, but with confidence in the authority Christ has given to His followers.

Stay attentive to the needs of the Person

At the same time, remain attentive to the person receiving ministry. Encourage them to stay engaged in the process through prayer, agreement with truth, and continued surrender to God. Deliverance is not something done to a person, but something they actively participate in as they turn toward Christ.

Peace and Truth

Throughout the ministry moment, maintain an atmosphere of peace and trust. The Holy Spirit is gentle and purposeful in His work. Allow Him to lead the pace of the process rather than attempting to control it yourself.

In every situation, remember that the goal of healing and deliverance is not merely the removal of spiritual oppression. The deeper purpose is restoration—helping individuals reconnect with God's truth, receive His love, experience His healing, and move forward in the freedom Christ has secured for them.

As Jesus promised:

*"So if the Son sets you free, you will be free indeed."
(John 8:36)*

HELPING THE PERSON WALK IN THEIR FREEDOM

When prayer for healing or deliverance has taken place, the ministry is not truly finished. One of the most important responsibilities you have as a minister is helping the individual understand how to continue walking in the freedom they have received.

Freedom is not only about what has been removed—it is also about what must now be established in its place. When areas of deception, spiritual oppression, or destructive patterns have been addressed, the person must begin filling their life with truth, healthy spiritual practices, and renewed ways of thinking.

Jesus spoke about the importance of what follows deliverance when He described a spirit leaving a person and later attempting to return. If the house remains empty, the situation can become worse than before.

"When an impure spirit comes out of a person… it goes and takes seven other spirits more wicked than itself, and they go in and live there." (Matthew 12:43–45)

This passage reminds us that freedom must be accompanied by transformation. The person who has received ministry must begin establishing new patterns that reinforce their relationship with God.

Encourage them to remain connected to Christ through prayer, worship, and time in Scripture. These practices help anchor the heart in truth and strengthen the individual's spiritual foundation.

It is also important for the person to remain connected to healthy Christian community. Isolation can often allow old patterns or lies to return, while supportive relationships provide encouragement, ac- countability, and continued growth.

You may also need to help the individual recognize and reject old lies if they attempt to resurface. Freedom often requires renewing the mind with God's truth.

Scripture reminds us of this transformation:

"Do not conform to the pattern of this world, but be transformed by the renewing of your mind." (Romans 12:2)

As they learn to replace old beliefs with the truth of God's Word, the foundation of their freedom becomes stronger.

Finally, remind them that freedom is sustained through ongoing dependence on the Holy Spirit. The same Spirit who brought healing and deliverance continues to guide, strengthen, and protect them as they move forward.

Your role as a minister is not to control their journey but to encourage them to remain rooted in Christ, where lasting freedom is found.

As they grow in their relationship with Him, the freedom they have received can deepen and become a testimony of God's restoring power.

A PRACTICAL FRAMEWORK FOR HEALING AND DELIVERANCE MINISTRY

Throughout this chapter we have explored the calling to help others experience healing and freedom through the power of Jesus Christ. We have considered the posture required for this work, the role of faith, the authority of Scripture, and the guidance of the Holy Spirit. We have also examined how spiritual bondage develops, the common doors through which it can enter, and the importance of discernment when ministering to others.

While every situation must ultimately be guided by the Holy Spirit, the principles discussed throughout this chapter often unfold in a recognizable pattern during healing and deliverance ministry. For this reason, it can be helpful to view the process through a simple frame- work that summarizes the steps commonly involved in guiding some- one toward freedom.

This framework does not replace the leading of the Holy Spirit. Rather, it gathers the principles already discussed into a practical over- view that can help ministers approach the work of restoration with clarity and wisdom.

Educate – Awareness Is the First Step Toward Change

As discussed earlier, many individuals come into ministry situations without fully understanding how spiritual strongholds develop or how freedom is established. Helping them understand the role of truth prepares their hearts for the work God desires to do. Jesus reminded His followers, *"Then you will know the truth, and the truth will set you free" (John 8:32).*

Education may include helping individuals understand topics such as deliverance, emotional healing, and survival patterns such as codependence, addiction, or trauma responses. In some cases, additional resources may be necessary to support these areas outside of the prayer or counseling session.

Assessment – Understanding the Whole Story

Before moving forward, ministers take time to listen carefully and understand the individual's experiences, struggles, and spiritual back- ground. As we have seen, not every struggle is purely spiritual, and wise ministry requires thoughtful listening and prayerful discernment.

It can be helpful to use an assessment tool that works for you or for the organization you represent. Understanding a person's history, spiritual background, relationships, and current needs provides valuable context for ministry. In many cases, encouraging individuals to write a life story—if they are able—can help reveal patterns and significant moments that shaped their journey.

Locate – Identifying Root Causes

As discussed in earlier sections on bondage and spiritual footholds, strongholds often develop around wounds, deception, trauma, or patterns of sin. Identifying these roots helps ensure that ministry addresses the true source of the struggle rather than merely treating the symptoms.

Locating these roots may require ongoing conversations, reflection exercises, or homework assignments that help the individual explore key behaviors, emotions, and relational patterns. Patience is important, as deeper causes often become clearer over time.

Test – Testing the Spirits

Scripture instructs believers to evaluate spiritual influences carefully: *"Do not believe every spirit, but test the spirits to see whether they are from God"* (1 John 4:1). This protects both the minister and the individual receiving ministry.

Testing a spirit may involve asking simple questions such as, "Do you believe Jesus is the Son of God?" or "Do you believe He died on the cross to save you from your sins?" Responses to these questions can sometimes reveal whether a spiritual influence is aligned with the truth of Christ.

Discern – Body, Soul, or Spirit

As explored earlier in the discussion on discernment, struggles may involve different dimensions of a person's life. Some issues originate in emotional wounds, unhealthy beliefs, or relational trauma, while others may involve spiritual oppression.

Discernment requires the guidance of the Holy Spirit and often operates as a spiritual gift. While helpful frameworks can assist in understanding patterns, true discernment ultimately comes through God's revelation. The Holy Spirit helps ministers see beyond what is merely presenting itself on the surface and understand what is actually taking place beneath it.

Soul Care – Healing the Wounds of the Heart

Many areas of bondage are connected to wounds carried in the heart. Inviting the Holy Spirit into these places allows truth to replace deception and healing to begin.

Soul care may involve processing grief and loss, identifying original wounds, understanding unhealthy relational entanglements, addressing unforgiveness, or confronting patterns of self-rejection. Because these areas often develop over many years, healing may unfold gradually over time rather than in a single moment.

Prayer – Bringing Everything Before the Lord

Prayer remains central throughout the entire process. Through prayer, individuals surrender wounds, confess sin, forgive others, renounce lies, and invite the Holy Spirit to restore what has been broken.

While the minister may guide the person through prayer, the focus must always remain on inviting the presence and authority of Jesus into the situation. At times prayer may involve quiet listening with the Holy Spirit so He can reveal deeper issues. In other moments, prayer may take the form of guided inner healing, intercession outside of the session, or simply waiting on God as He works in the individual's heart.

Deliverance – Addressing Spiritual Opposition

When spiritual oppression is present, deliverance prayer may be necessary. Through the authority of Jesus Christ, opposing spiritual influences are commanded to leave and the believer's freedom in Christ is affirmed.

Deliverance should always be approached with humility, calm confidence, and complete reliance upon the Holy Spirit. The goal is never dramatic confrontation but the quiet exercise of Christ's authority. There are many forms of deliverance prayer, but the central focus remains the same: bringing the individual into the freedom that Jesus has already secured through His death and resurrection.

.Ongoing Maintenance – Walking in Freedom

Freedom must be nurtured through continued spiritual growth. Individuals should be encouraged to renew their minds with Scripture, cultivate habits of prayer and worship, and remain connected to healthy Christian community.

As believers continue walking in truth and intimacy with God, the freedom they have received becomes established and sustained.

Over time, the life that was once marked by bondage becomes a testimony of God's restoring grace and life changing power.

Understanding these areas helps those ministering deliverance recognize where spiritual influence may have gained access. When these doors are brought into the light and addressed through repentance, forgiveness, and truth, the ground that once allowed oppression can be reclaimed through the authority of Jesus Christ.

This understanding prepares those involved in ministry to move carefully and prayerfully into the process of helping individuals walk out of bondage into freedom.

A FINAL COMMISSION

Throughout this book we have explored how Christ brings freedom into the life of the believer—breaking the power of sin, healing wound- ed places of the heart, and restoring what the enemy has sought to destroy. Yet the work of freedom does not end with personal restoration. God often uses those who have experienced His freedom to help others find it as well.

The mission of Jesus did not end when He ascended to the Father. Through the presence of the Holy Spirit, His work continues through those who follow Him. As believers walk in faith and obedience, they become instruments through which His compassion, truth, and authority reach a world that desperately needs restoration.

This calling may take many forms. Some may serve in counseling, pastoral care, prayer ministry, or healing and deliverance. Others will simply walk faithfully with those God places in their path—offering wisdom, encouragement, and prayer to those who are struggling.

What matters most is not the title of the ministry but the posture of the heart. Those who remain surrendered to Christ, attentive to the Holy Spirit, and grounded in His Word become vessels through which His life flows to others.

The work of freedom ultimately belongs to God. Yet in His mercy, He invites His people to participate in what He is doing. As you continue walking with Christ, remain rooted in His presence, faithful in your own growth, and willing to serve wherever He leads. When you do, the freedom you have received will begin to reach others who are still searching for hope.

Reflection

As you come to the end of this journey, take a moment to reflect on what God may be revealing to you.

1. Where has He brought freedom into your own life?

2. What truths has He used to reshape the way you see yourself, others, or Him?
3. What areas of healing has He begun restoring in your heart?

Often the places where God has worked most deeply in our own lives become the very places where He equips us to help others.

Ask the Lord to guide your steps as you continue walking with Him. Remain attentive to His voice, faithful in your growth, and willing to respond when He invites you to participate in His work of restoration.

A Closing Prayer
Heavenly Father,

Thank You for the freedom that comes through Jesus Christ. Thank You for Your Word that brings truth and for the Holy Spirit who provides power and leads us into healing and restoration.

Continue to guide us as we walk with You. Teach us to remain humble, attentive to Your voice, and faithful in the calling You place before us.

Where there is still brokenness within us, bring Your healing. Where there is fear, replace it with faith. Where there is confusion, lead us into truth. Use our lives to reflect Your love and grace so that those who are bound may find freedom and those who are wounded may find restoration.

We surrender ourselves again to Your purposes. In the name of Jesus, Amen.

RESOURCES

Tucker Counseling

Tucker Counseling provides theocentric (God-centered) counseling designed to help individuals address the deeper roots of emotional, spiritual, and behavioral struggles. This counseling approach integrates biblical truth, spiritual discernment, and practical guidance to help individuals understand the influences shaping their beliefs, emotions, and behaviors.

Through decades of counseling and ministry experience, Tucker Counseling helps individuals uncover the root causes of destructive patterns and begin a process of lasting transformation.

Tucker Counseling offers individual counseling as well as a structured 90-Day Online Freedom Program, designed to guide participants through a process of personal healing, spiritual growth, and renewal of the mind. A marriage program is available to bring personal and marital healing.

The ministry also provides spiritual warfare and deliverance prayer ministry, helping individuals address spiritual strongholds and influences that may contribute to ongoing struggles.

Learn more at:
www.TuckerCounseling.com
Email: robert@tuckercounseling.com | 866.543.3361

Living Free Institute

Living Free Institute provides Christ-centered training and ministry programs designed to equip individuals and leaders with tools for emotional healing, spiritual freedom, and personal transformation.

The Institute offers a unique 7-Day Healing Intensive that helps participants identify the deeper roots of emotional pain, destructive patterns, and spiritual struggles while guiding them through a process of healing and restoration.

Living Free Institute also offers coaching and ministry training programs designed to equip individuals to help others walk through the journey of healing and transformation.

Learn more at:
www.LivingFreeInstitute.com

OTHER BOOKS PUBLISHED BY LIVING FREE INSTITUTE

Living Free Institute also provides additional Christ-centered resources designed to help individuals grow in healing, freedom, and spiritual maturity.

The Christian Codependence Recovery Workbook
by Stephanie Tucker

Christian Families in Recovery
by Robert Tucker and Stephanie Tucker

A House that Grace Built
by Stephanie Tucker

Boundaries and Breaking Cycles of Pain
by Stephanie Tucker

The Book of Job: Misunderstood
by Stephanie Tucker

For free devotionals and other resources, visit:
www.LivingFreeInstitute.com

www.ingramcontent.com/pod-product-compliance
Lightning Source LLC
Chambersburg PA
CBHW051759050726
47598CB00006B/2352